A book of inspiration and motivation

OBSTACLES

A STEPPING STONE FOR SUCCESS

"Your birth is a miracle
Your existence is for a cause
Your thought, word and deed be nobler
Your life is a motivation
Your death should be an inspiration"

PROFESSOR N. PALANI

BlueRose
Publishers

First Published in January 2020

ISBN: 978-93-89888-18-8

BLUEROSE PUBLISHERS

www.bluerosepublishers.com

info@bluerosepublishers.com

+91 8882 898 898

Cover Design:

Mohit Joshi

Typographic Design:

Tanya Raj Upadhyay

Distributed by: BlueRose, Amazon, Flipkart, Shopclues

This book is dedicated to

My wife Mrs. S. Dhanalakshmi who
has stood up by my side
in all my endevours

and

Dr Paul Brand for his encouragement

EPILOGUE

Life is not a bed of roses, but how you make it meaningful matters the most. In my case, this is what happened. I was born in Samalkot, in Andhra Pradesh, India in 1936. My life began with innumerable sufferings and now, I am a renowned physiotherapist. My father, Shri T. G Narasimhan was working at the Indian Railways. He was suffering from pneumonia and passed away in 1942 at the age of 32 at Vijayawada Railway Hospital, Andhra Pradesh. My mother, Mrs Sarada was mentally affected by the incident. I also had three sisters.

My paternal uncle, Shri T. G. Krishnasamy sympathised with our family and brought us to Vellore, our native place. He got me enrolled at a school there. One day, Dr R. G. Cochrane, a medical expert from CMC Hospital, Vellore, had come to our school for free medical check-up of all the students. When he examined me, he found a few white patches on my skin and declared that I was suffering from leprosy. He advised me to discontinue my education at Vellore and get treated at a leprosy sanatoriumin Chenglepet, Tamil Nadu, India.

At the sanatorium, I was admitted in the boarding room no. 6 which was the place for younger children to stay.

I started attending the school while staying at the sanatorium for the treatment of leprosy. In those days, it was very difficult to treat leprosy. Luckily, I was completely cured of it in 1946 and returned to Vellore. After returning, I assisted my uncle in his grocery business. After a few months, my uncle enrolled me at a high school to continue my studies.

After completing high school, I started working in Vellore at Christian Medical College Hospital(CMCH) as a physiotherapy assistant and got a stipend of Rs. 20/- per month. I was fortunate enough to complete my high school studies and the physiotherapy course at CMC Hospital itself. To be employed as a physiotherapist there was another blessing.

I had the fortune of working with world-famous Dr. Paul Brand in the 1950s, who worked at CMC Hospital, Vellore. His discoveries and methods of treating leprosy are followed throughout the world to date. I was associated with eminent personalities like Dr. Paul Brand, Dr. A. J. Selvapandiyan, Dr. Fritschi, Dr. S. Karat, Prof. T. N. Jagadesan, Dr. C. K. Job, Dr. K. V. Desikan, and Dr. Mary Verghese. I also got to meet great personalities like Vinobabave, Baba Amte, Dr. Sushila Naiyar, Group Capitan Cheshire, and others.

I would like to offer my sincere gratitude to CMC hospital, Vellore for giving me the opportunity to work at the institution and also to Dr. Paul Brand who encouraged me to write the book to motivate the future generation. I also want to thank my wife, S. Dhanalakshmi, my daughters, Er. P. Vasughi and Dr. P. Kalaivani, and Mr. Munireddy for helping me to write this book.

This book not only talks about my work with leprosy patients but also of my vast experience in the field of physiotherapy. This book describes the methods/techniques to deal with the day to day ailments like back pain, knee pain, neck pain, diabetes, obesity, etc.

This book is about my life time work in the field of physiotherapy, particularly aboutthe treatment of leprosy patients, and how I converted my obstacles into stepping stones towards success.

PROFESSOR – N. PALANI.

FORMERLY HEAD PHYSIOTHERAPY EDUCATION
CHRISTIAN MADICAL COLLAGE – VELLORE.

Director Vinayaka Missions Collage of Physiotherapy

Salem

CELL: 9629851191

Prof. V. CHOCKALINGAM

M.D. (Med.) D.M. (Cardiology), F.I.S.E. (IND)
F.C.C.P., F.I.C.A., F.A.C.C., (U.S.A.), M.N.A.M.S.
(Cardiology), D.Sc.,
Emeritus Professor, Cardiology.
Dr. MGR Medical University, Chennai.

25. Taylors Road, Kilpauk, Chennai - 600 010.
Phone : Res. : 26441717, Clinic : 26426565
Mobile : 98410 91717
E-mail : drveecee27@ymail.com

17.05.2019

FOREWORD

It gives me indeed a great pleasure to write a foreword for the book «Obstacles-A stepping stone.

Prof. N. Palani is a distinguished physiotherapist and a teacher. He has trained hundreds of physiotherapists who are working in India and abroad. He is also a recipient of a number of awards including fellowship award in 1990 at Mumbai.

He received the best citizen of India award along with the late prime minister Vajbai and Dr Manmohan Singh in 2002. Mahatma Gandhi was a great inspiration in his life and he had seen him in 1946. In his early childhood, he underwent innumerable sufferings which he had overcome successfully and considers them as a stepping stone for his success in life.

He had worked with the world famous Dr.Paul Brand for a number of years in his leprosy research team. He has been associated with great personalities like with Shri.Baba Amte, Dr.Sushila Nayyar Group Captain Chesire , Vinobhaba bave, Dr. Mary Verghese, and others.

Mr.Palani had presented a number of papers at national and international conferences and has a few articles published in medical journals to his credit. He isrecognised as a eminent physiotherapist and served as a Member of Board of studies Dr MGR Medical University, Shri Ramachandra medical college , Chennai and Vinayaga Missions Medical College Salem. This book also gives simple remedies for tackling problems related to joint pain in ageing and emphasis the need of exercising the joint while growing old.

Health by definition is not a disease free stage, it is a positive state of health mentally, Physically, spiritually and socially thereby - **Holistic.**

For our **E**xistence -**E^3**: **Emotion, Eating, Exercise.** The three mantras one should follow to live more than 100 years of healthy life.

1. Be positive in thinking
2. Be Healthy in eating
3. Be adequate in exercising

Prof.N.Palani is giving all the above elements for his fellow persons by his many decades of experience.

Keep moving in relation to space and time for you to “Live Life Better”.

I wish him all success in his future endevaours.

Prof. V. CHOCKALINGAM

Early Beginning

I was born in 1936 in Samalkot, Andhra Pradesh. My early memories are the ones of my house – a railway quarter in Tenali. I had a sister, Papi, who was two years elder than me and two more sisters, Kantha and Parvathi, younger by one and half years each. I remember that my mother, Saradawas very beautiful and used to sing well. My father, Narasimhan, workedat the Indian Railways and used to take all of us frequently on tours. I remember having visited Madurai, Chennai, Rameswaram, Thanjavur, Chidambaram, Vadalur, etc. at a very young age. He was a pious man and used to pray regularly. He was a devotee of Vallalar and had become a vegetarian following Saint Vallalar's principles. He taught me to speak and write in English. He believed in compassion towards animals.

My father T. G. Narasimhan

My father was a hardworking man. In Tenali, he created a small garden in front of our house and made a fence for it out of bamboo sticks to protect the plants. He had planted banana saplings and vegetable plants in the garden. We would use vegetables from the garden for cooking.

When my father went to purchase provisions for the kitchen, I used to accompany him. In those days, things were cheap. We could buy 20 kg of rice for just one rupee. Even fruits and vegetables were affordable.

One day, my father and I were travelling to Vijayawada city by train, passing over the river Krishna. As the train passed through the bridge, people started throwing coins into the river as a symbol of worship to God for giving them the river for their needs.

My father made me join a primary school in Tenali. At school, I learnt to read Telugu. Our teacher made us read our lessons loudly to get the pronunciations correct. I still remember that whenever the sound of recitation decreased in the class, the teacher would beat the children one by one with a stick until the sound improved.

At Tenali, daily, I had to cross a railway line to reach the school. One day, as I was crossing the railway line, a high-speed train just crossed me narrowly. I was stunned for a minute and my father, who saw this from a distance, started shouting at me for being careless.

We had a well in our house from which we used to fetch water. One day, I saw a tortoise in our well. I was amused by the tortoise as it used to appear and disappear frequently in the water. With an intention to play with the tortoise, I tied a rope to the bucket and dropped it into the well. I made the tortoise get into the bucket and got it outside the well. My father saw this and got furious. He beat me for being cruel to the tortoise and advised me not to do such things toanimals in the future.

My uncle T. G. Krishnaswamy

During the year 1942, my father fell ill with pneumonia at Tenali. He succumbed to the fever as there was no proper cure for the disease in those days because penicillin was not widely used in India. He knew that he was about to die and called all of us and cried as he felt that he would be leaving his family at a very early age. He passed away when he was just32 years old. He left behind four small children and my mother who was mentally ill.

My grandfather, paternal uncle, and few other relatives had come for his funeral at Vijayawada

Railway Hospital. As my mother had mental illness, she could not understand that my father had passed away, and the way she was fanning my father's body with a handmade fan melted everybody's heart. My father's cremation was held at a burial ground on the banks of river Krishna. My paternal uncle T. G. Krishnasamy, sympathized with us and brought us to Vellore, which is our native place.

My uncle made me join an elementary school for my studies at Vellore. One day after the school was over, I had come home and people around me informed me that my mother had left the house with my sisters as she wanted to get back to our house at the Tenali Railway Quarters. She had walked about10 km away from our residence. Fortunately, a person known to our family saw them and brought them back

At school, I continued my studies. During the same year 1942, one day, a world-famous doctor, Dr. R. G Cochrane came from CMC Hospital, Vellore, to conduct free medical check-up of all the students in our school. When he examined me, he noticed a few white patches on my body and diagnosed that I was suffering from leprosy. He also advised me that I had to stop my studies at school and suggested that I should be admitted to a leprosy sanatorium at Chengelpet, Tamil Nadu, and get myself treated.

He came to my house and advised our elders to be aware of the importance of curing leprosy. He even advised them to take immediate action in this regard. Accordingly, my uncle arranged for my admission at Chengelpet leprosy sanatorium so that I could get treated.

Leprosy

In 1873, Dr. Hansen discovered that leprosy is caused by microbacteriumleprae. In older times, people had the impression that leprosy was an incurable disease and a result of the curse of God, illegal sexual relations, heredity or accumulated sins of the previous birth. Those who were affected by the disease had to live without any hope of future as there was no proper treatment available and they were considered as outcasts of the society.

Dr. Hansen

Many of the leprosy patients had deformities of hands and feet. They were considered as unworthy citizens and were thrown out by their family members. As a result, many leprosy patients had to beg for a living. They slept on the roadside as their families had disowned them. They were treated as outcasts and had to live without any job.

Worse than this was that the patients had to endure undue suffering in many parts of the globe. During the1930s, leprosy patients in Japan were segregated and made to stay throughout their lifetime, in a secluded sanatorium far away from the city. In 1937, China, eighty leprosy patients were shot dead and pushed into a limestone well. The overall situation of leprosy patients was pathetic as nobody cared for them.

In 1940, a new dawn arose for leprosy patients. It was discovered that leprosy patients felt better when chaulmoogra oil was injected into their tissues. In 1950, with the invention of DAPSONE tablet, a cure for leprosy was born. However, the tablets acted very slowly and leprosy patients had to consume it for years to get completely cured.

In 1981, leprosy treatment underwent a complete transformation when amulti-drug therapy was introduced. It was a blessing that these medicines viz. , DAPSONE, RIFAMPICIN, and CLOFIZIMINE together could act on leprosy bacteria and kill it at a faster rate. Even patients with the disease in advanced stages could be treated and completely cured if they consumed these drugs continuously for one year. In case of patients who are minimally affected by leprosy, a complete cure is possible within the span of a few months. As this disease is widely prevalent in India, China, Bangladesh, Indonesia, and African countries, the World Health Organisation supplies these medicines free of cost to all these nations.

The irony is that the symptoms of this disease are visible only five years after the organism has affected the person. Though leprosy is not a highly contagious disease, it is found that if a person moves very close to an infected patient who is not taking treatment, there are chances that the disease can infect that person too. If the disease is identified in the initial stage itself and treated with multi-drug therapy, the patient can be completely cured and will be protected from developing deformity. But as there is a stigma attached to the disease and fear among people, many of the affected persons do not come for treatment at the initial stage. A change in the mind-set of the common public is needed and awareness needs to be created to prevent /overcome this disease. If leprosy patients approach doctors for treatment without any fear and hesitation in the initial stage itself, they can be cured perfectly without deformation and can avoid a lot of emotional trauma and agony.

Initial Symptoms of Leprosy

(A) White patches appearing on any part of the body.

(B) No pain sensation in any part of the body.

(C) Swelling of the nerves.

If a person tests positive for leprosy by means of lab tests, the individual should immediately approach a doctor for treatment. Early in the 1950s, members of Gandhi Memorial Leprosy Foundation, Wardha, went door to door throughout the country and surveyed the prevalence of leprosy in the region. If the disease was detected, they made arrangements for continuous treatment of the patient. Laterin 1955, the government of India undertook similar action throughout the country. The World Health Organization also followed this procedure in various countries and made leprosy treatment available for a larger number of people free of cost.

Nowadays, leprosy patients are not kept isolated and they are given treatment in the main stream, along with the other patients. Now, the patients come regularly to the hospital without any hesitation. If tribes living in secluded mountainous areas and people living in remote villages are diagnosed with leprosy, they are given proper treatment too. Complete eradication of leprosy is possible in India.

Though research for finding vaccination for leprosy is going on worldwide, no vaccination has been invented for prevention of this disease so far.

In the 1960s, it was found that 2% of the population was affected by leprosy. To reduce this large number, paramedical workers went from door to door and tested everyone; identified leprosy patients and started giving treatment to them. This method has been successful to a large extent.

The World Health Organization made an assessment and declared that only 0. 01% of the population is affected by leprosy. The multi-drug therapy [DAPSONE, RIFAMPICIN, and CLOFIZIMINE] not only kills leprosy bacteria but also prevents the disease from spreading. Hence, chances are bright for the complete eradication of leprosy.

My Treatment at Chengulpet Leprosy Sanatorium:

Dr. R. G. Cochrane

In 1942, as per the advice of Dr. R. G. Cochrane, my uncle arranged for my admission at Lady Wellington Leprosy Sanatorium, at Chengulpet which is now called CLTRI[Central Leprosy Teaching and Research Institute]. This is a special hospital for the treatment of leprosy patients. On admission, they made incisions(tiny cuts) at twelve places in my body with a scalpel blade and extracted smears from the cuts and tested them under the microscope for leprosy organisms. It was found that I was infected with leprosy.

I was admitted in boarding room no. 6 which was the place for small children to stay. I was given a dhoti, a banyan, an aluminium plate, a mug, a mat to sleep on and a black blanket. I remember that my identity number was 99. We were given rice porridge as breakfast. At noon, we had rice, sambar, buttermilk and vegetable subji. Every evening at six, dinner was provided. All of us used to stand in a queue to get the food and after eating, we used to clean our plates.

I remember that one of the inmate sat the boarding school took me around the hospital and showed me the ward for chronic patients. At the chronic ward, most of the patients were aged and many of them had crippling deformities of their hands and feet. They were able to move from one place to another by crawling and some of them were blind. On seeing them, I was deeply distressed and depressed. It was an agonizing experience to witness such a sight because in those days, medical treatment was not available as is today and leprosy, unlike today, was not completely curable. I was in a pit of distress in the midst of an encircling gloom from where I could not get away from the feeling of such an agonising experience. I went on weeping for days together, lonely as a cloud with an experience of aloneness of the alone.

Boarding room where I stayed 70 years back

The inmate added to my agony by saying that this will be our fate and we would have to go through all the suffering. I also saw a patient who passed away and they were carrying him for cremation. Having lost my father, my mother being mentally ill and myself being away from my family, my life became quite miserable.

The institution was highly disciplined and I was attending school regularly in 1942. 'Early to bed and early to rise' were the guiding principles. Study hours were allotted and prayers were conducted every day before going to bed. I took interest in sports such as 100 meter running, football, carom, chess, etc. , and all these factors helped to lessen my worries.

Every Saturday morning, all of us had to take an oil-bath by applying chaulmoogra oil to the entire body. A circus was organised for young children. After applying oil on our bodies, we had to climb on another person's shoulders. That person used to walk very fast around the ground. Every time we had this activity, I was petrified of falling down.

Finally, at the end of the session, a human pyramid formation was made (a few boys would stand on the shoulders of other boys) and myself being the youngest, I was made to stand on the top. The thought of being made to stand at the top of so many boys used to terrorise me everytime.

During my stay at the boarding centre in Chengulpet, about 20 boys were admitted. Even during the cold season, we had to bathe in cold water so that we could withstand the cold climate. During the rainy season, there used to be tiny waterfalls in the nearby hills. I remember having enjoyed bathing under those waterfalls.

Under the leadership of Dr. COCHRANE, the Chengulpet Lady Wellington Leprosy Sanatorium did yeoman services for leprosy patients by treating them.

Leprosy:

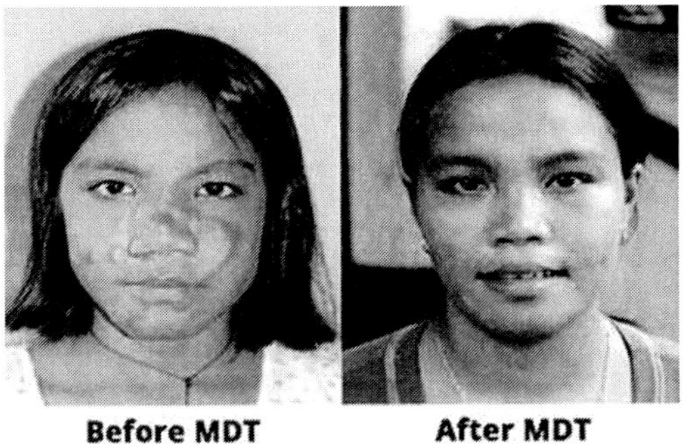

Before Treatment After Treatment.

During my stay at Chengulpet , my uncle, T. G. Krishnasamy used to send me a money order of two rupees every month. In the institution, we were given only rice porridge in the mornings. The money that my uncle sent was very valuable for me because I used to buy a glass of milk and two idlis every day with them. I was one of the few fortunate people there to receive this sum. I remember that I would use those two rupees for buying soap and tooth powder also because the cost of living was cheap in those days.

When I was at the sanatorium for treatment, I had the privilege of seeing the Father of our nation, Mr. M. K Gandhi. In 1946, Mahatma Gandhi was visiting South India and the train was made to stop at Thirumani near our institute. I remember Mahatma Gandhi offering namaste with folded hands to all the leprosy patients who had gathered there. However, he did not speak a single word as it was his day of silence. As I was a young boy, I did not know the greatness of Mahatma Gandhi in those days.

Mahatma Gandhi

I did not realize the importance of Mahatma Gandhiuntil I read his autobiography in my 20's. When I read the autobiography, I was touched by his greatness.

In his autobiography, he tells the story of Harishchandra who had createda great impact on him and was a majorinspiration in his life.

HARISHCHANDRA:

In the story, King Harishchandra, come whatever may in his life, was determined to speak onlythe truth and had laid it down as a principle in his life. Saint Vishvamitratries every trick to make him break his vow. Because of his principle, Harishchandra had to lose his wife, his son, and his kingdom. Harishchandra, with no money in his hands, was forced to sell his wife and son to a Brahmin to pay for the debts. When the money that was collected did not suffice, he sold himself to a guard at the cremation ground. Harishchandra was collecting taxes for the dead bodies to be cremated.

Harishchandra selling his wife and son to a Brahmin.

Harishchandra, his wife, and his son had to sustain tremendous hardships while doing their respective jobs. Harishchandra worked at the cremation ground by cremating dead bodies while his wife and son became domestic helpers at the house of the Brahmin. One day, the son went to the garden to pluck flowers for his master's prayer. There, he was bitten by a snake and died instantly. His mother, having nobody to sympathise with her, carried the dead body to the cremation grounds. In acute poverty, she could not even pay the taxes needed to cremate her son. Harishchandra did not recognise his wife and son. He asked the lady to sell her gold neck chain and pay the tax. It was at this instance that his wife recognized the man as her husband as she had a boon that her husband alone could see the chain. Harishchandra, then came to her and recognized her. He became deeply distressed with agony.

Harishchandra, Chandiramathi, and Vishvamitra

But, Harishchandra was bound by his duty. He could perform the cremation only after the acceptance of tax. So, he asked his wife if she was willing to face further hardships and stand by him in his hour of calamity. The faithful wife readily agreed. She had in her possession only a *saree*, a part of which was used to cover the dead body of her son. She offered half of her only dress as the tax which Harishchandra accepted and performed the last rites of their son.

Lord Vishnu, Indra, all the Devas, and sage Vishwamitra manifested at the scene and praised Harishchandra for his truthfulness, perseverance, and steadfastness. They brought his son back to life. They also offered the king and his wife instant places in the heaven.

In my opinion, the writer of Harishchandra is greater than a scientist because his objective was to build up the character of the people. If the character is good, the rest follows. This story is the basic foundation on which Gandhji had built up his character and served the people of India and the world at large.

Shravan Kumarand his aged parents(Ramayana):

One more story which was close to Gandhijiwas that of Shravan Kumar, a mythological character in the Ramayana.

It is a Hindu belief that pilgrimage to various shrines and holy places undertaken in old-age purifies the soul. Hence, Shravan Kumar's parents told him that they had become quite aged and they, therefore, wanted him to take them to various places of pilgrimage.

Shravan Kumar carrying his parents on a pilgrimage.

Those were the days when means of transportation were scarce and costly. As Shravan Kumar could not afford it, he decided to carry his parents in two baskets, which could be placed on a stick on his shoulders. He took a strong bamboo stick, and at its ends, he tied two baskets with strong ropes. He placed his father in one of the baskets and his mother in the other. Shravanand his parents started their pilgrimage.

According to Ramayana, while hunting in the forest of Ayodhya, King Dashratha heard a sound near a lake. He thought that an animal was drinking water from the lake and released an arrow to hunt it. When he crossed the lake to collect the animal, unfortunately, he found that his arrow had struck a boy who was bleeding. The boy was Shravan Kumar. He told Das h ratha that he had come to the lake to collect water for his sick and aged parents who were both blind and he had been carrying them on a bamboo stick. He requested the king to take water to his parents. After telling his tale, Shravan died. The king took water to Shravan's parents and told them of his tragic mistake. The poor parents were unable to bear the shock. They cursed Dashratha that he too would experience the same kind of grief in his future.

The above story emphasizes one's devotion and love for parents. Mahatma Gandhi was deeply influenced by the virtues of telling the truth when he watched the play of Harishchandra in his childhood and devotion to parents by reading Shravan Kumar's story.

India has given birth to great people like Tulsidas, Valmiki, Buddha, Vivekananda, and many others. We also have teachings of godly people like Jesus Christ and Prophet Muhammad. We try to imbibe good qualities from their teachings so that every spirit can be improved.

My Schooling

I was discharged from the leprosy hospital in 1946, after four years of treatment. I was also given a certificate stating that I was not infectious. After coming to Vellore in 1946, I used to go to my uncle's shop to support him. My uncle had a good heart and he arranged for me to continue my education at a high school.

After getting discharged from Chengelpet, I continued to have chalmoogra oil injections at CMC, Vellore, to prevent the disease from relapsing. I continued this procedure for many years. The injection room at CMCH was at the corner of the hospital. I used to feel uneasy and worried because anyone could see me going there for treatment and the stigma attached to leprosy was very prevalent in those days.

As I was prompt in taking medicines and injections, I did not get deformation in any part of my body.

While I was studying at the school, one of my classmates remarked that I had been suffering from leprosy and was having injections at CMCH. He said it in the midst of a group of students. I carefully diverted the topic and led the conversation to something else because there was so much stigma associated with leprosy in those days.

My uncle

My uncle, T. G. Krishnasamy had a business of rice, jaggery, tamarind, etc. at Vellore. After school, every day, I used to go to the market and collect the dues from other merchants to help my uncle.

His wife, Mrs. Seetha Lakshmi, was an innocent and kind woman who loved all of us. We all lived together till both of them passed away. My other uncle, T. G. Govindaraju enrolled me in Donbosco high school, Vellore, and was instrumental for my education. I also remember that while studying at Donbosco Higher Secondary School, my uncle, T. G. Krishnasamy used to give me seven silver one-rupee coins as school term fees.

I had a close friend called Janakiraman who lived close to my house. Both of us used to go to school together every day.

Vellore Fort

In the evening, we used to play together. During holidays, we used to go to Vellore Fort and other hills to play and study together. Half way to the hill range, there was a broad rock. We both used to sit there and read our lessons. In those days, children did not carry water bottle along with them. Whenever Jankiraman and I felt thirsty, we used to squeeze the cactus fruit growing on the hill sides and quench our thirst. It was a game for us.

During the summer vacation, in the month of May, I would go to my uncle's shop and help him. He used to send me to wholesale shops to bring samples of groundnuts, tamarind, jaggery and different varieties of lentils. I was also to take down the rates from the wholesale shops so that my uncle could procure and sell the items. He used to buy good quality products and send them to places like Mayavaram, Cuddalore, and Panruti. I was sent home everyday at noon to bring lunch in a tiffin box for him. In those days only a few people could afford chappals(slippers). The distance between our home and my uncle's shop was nearly three kms. It was difficult to walk bare feet for such a long distance in the hot sun. So, wherever I found trees on the way, I would stand under the shade for some time and then continue. At night, I would return home late along with the other workers of the shop.

Dr. IDA SCUDDAR

Dr. IDA SCUDDAR, an American lady, started the CMC Hospital at Vellore in the year 1900. It was started as a one bed hospital at that time. But now, the hospital has gained international fame and people from every nook and corner of India come to CMCH for specialised and quality medical treatment. Madam Ida Scudder's family had lived in India and served this country for three generations. When Ida Scudder was young, she used to feel sad about the poor living conditions of people of India and the diseases prevalent here. She studied at Massachusetts University and returned to India to take care of hersick mother in 1890.

During those days, pregnancy and childbirth used to be a nightmare for women as deliveries were conducted by unqualified maids and any complication during childbirth led to the death of the mother or the child. No qualified female gynaecologist was available for monitoring the deliveries and the Indian women shunned from the male doctors. One night, she saw three pregnant ladies dying one after another because there was no lady doctor available to conduct the deliveries.

At that moment, Ida Scudder realised the purpose of her life and strongly felt that God has created her in order to serve the poor Indian women. In 1899, she studied medicine at the Kernel Medical College, New York, and started a small hospital in Vellore. She did not get married and dedicated her entire life time to work as a doctor. Later, her hospital grew into a multi-speciality world famous institution– the CMC Hospital at Vellore. It has served thousands of people till date.

Joining CMCH, Vellore

CMC Hospital, Vellore

After completing my basic education at the school, as I could not afford college education, I joined the CMC Hospital as a leprosy technician trainee with a meagre stipend of Rs. 20.

I did my training under Miss Ruth Thomas, a British physiotherapist who had come to India to treat leprosy patients. She used to take my classes daily of Anatomy, Physiology, and other leprosy related subjects. I remember that I used to collect bones from the graveyard for my anatomy classes. Later, Miss Ruth Thomas joined the SLR Leprosy Hospital at Karigiri. After completing my work in the morning at CMC Hospital, I used to take my bicycle and travel for30 Kms up and down to the SLR hospital at Karigiri to attend her classes.

Working with Dr. Paul Brand:

Dr. Paul Brand

Dr. Paul brand was born in India. His parents were working as missionaries in Kolli hills near Salem and cared for the tribal people in the hilly areas. They also used to teach modern methods of agriculture, carpentry, poultry, etc, to the tribal people living in those areas. At the age of nine, Dr. Paul Brand was sent to England for further education. He got trained in carpentry and learnt masonry work as well. When he got an opportunity through a missionary organization to study medicine, he joined a medical college and completed his FRCS in England. He also served as a surgeon in WWII for a brief period. On the invitation of Dr. R. G. Cockrane, he came from England and joined as a surgeon at CMCH, Vellore. Dr. R. G. Cockrane requested him to do reconstructive surgery of leprosy patients. In those days, doctors were not willing even to touch the hands of leprosy patients. However, Dr. Paul Brand accepted the challenge and started assessing the deformed hands and feet of the patients and started their treatment.

Dr. Paul Brand examining a leprosy patient

He started his work on tendon transfers for leprosy patients to correct the deformities of hands and feet. Dr. Paul Brand mastered the techniques and ultimately became one of the leading authorities of tendon transfers and rehabilitation programmes of leprosy patients in the world.

Dr. Paul Brand was also interested in treating ulcers. Many leprosy patients do not have any sensation of pain. When they walk barefoot, many times, thorns or glass pieces pierce the sole of their feet. In a matter of a few days, they get open wounds on their feet.

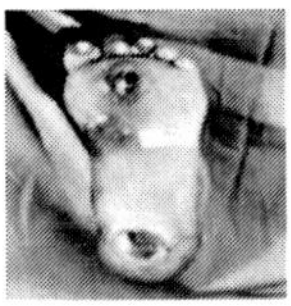	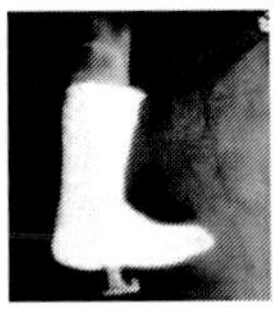	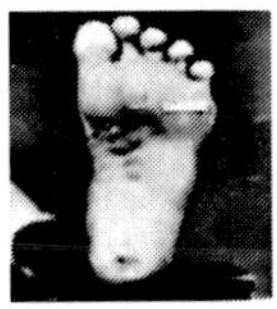	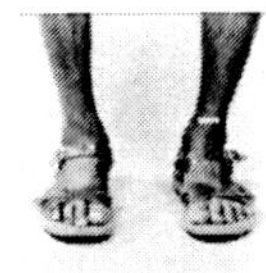
Foot with Ulcer	**Plaster Cast**	**Same foot after healing**	**MCR footwear to prevent ulcer**

Dr. Paul Brand did a number of experiments on ulcer treatment with antibiotics. He did not succeed in healing these ulcers until one day when he applied a plaster of Paris cast to a leprosy patient for the healing of his ulcer. The patient was asked to come after six weeks for the removal of the cast. This was the first case when he had treated a leprosy patient with ulcer using plaster of Paris. When Dr. Paul Brand was removing the cast, I was standing near him and saw that the ulcer had healed completely. I was greatly surprised and felt that a miracle has happened.

A teacher who was working at a school was infected by leprosy and had come for treatment with a very severe ulcer in his foot. He was in immense agony and told Dr. Brand that he was on the verge of losing his job due to his ulcer. An X-ray was taken and it was found that there were a number of fractures in his foot. In spite of broken bones, the patient had been walking because he couldn't feel any pain. This might have been the reason why Dr. Brand once said, "Pain is a gift of God". The patient was admitted in the ward for ulcer treatment.

Few more plaster casts were applied and by the end of eight weeks, his ulcers were fully healed. Dr. Paul Brand suggested the teacher to wear suitable MCR footwear to prevent recurrence of the ulcer. The patient was extremely happy. He went back to his place and resumed work as a school teacher.

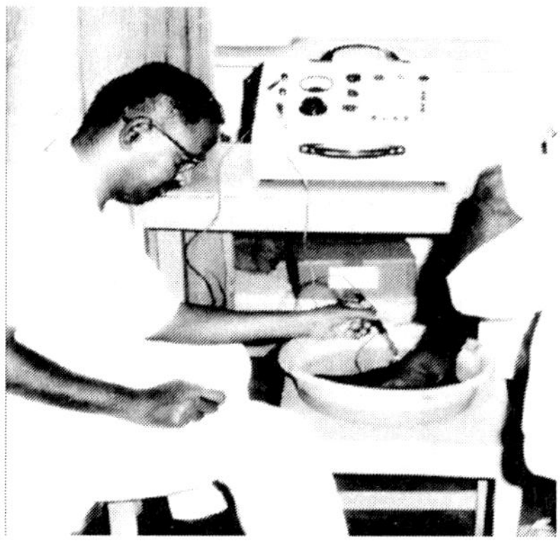

Author giving electrical treatment to a leprosy patient

Whenever he used to refer patients for surgery, I was supposed to prepare the hand for surgery and carry out the pre and post-operative treatment of their deformities, for proper functioning of the hand and to make the hands more useful.

One day, a young lady patient who had leprosy, came for treatment. Both her hands were deformed and non-functional. She was a dancer. Dr. Paul Brand asked me to prepare her stiff hands by doing physiotherapy and asked me to prepare her for surgery. When her hands were ready for surgery, he did the tendon transfers and asked me to carry out the post-operative physiotherapy for her. Her hands became really beautiful after surgery, followed by physiotherapy treatment. She was asked to dance and I remember that later, a small rehabilitation film titled **Lifted Hands** was made. This film won an international award.

It was difficult to work with Dr. Paul Brand without sufficient knowledge which could be discussed with him technically. I worked hard to acquire that knowledge and skill. Having seen my work when the WHO Doctors had come to visit Vellore, Dr. Brand used to depute me to take them to the ward, and explain to them about the condition of the patients.

Dr. Paul Brand appreciating the boy Toy made by the patient.

One day, late in the evening, I got into his car, as he usually dropped me near to the CMC eye hospital which was close to my residence. On our way, he said that he had been operating for the whole day with no food and felt terribly hungry. I had some tender coconut in my lunch box, soI asked him if he would be interested in eating the same. Without any hesitation, he happily took the tender coconut and ate it to his satisfaction.

I told Dr. Paul Brand that it was quite amazing to see those ulcers get healed with plaster treatment and the work should be spread on a national level so that it benefits a larger number of patients. I suggested that we create a basic leprosy physiotherapy technician course to teach how to apply plaster to heal the ulcers, followed by MCR footwear. Dr. Paul Brand took the initiative and contacted Professor T. N Jagadisan, the Organizing Secretary of the Indian Leprosy Association.

Professor T. N Jagadisan

Professor T. N Jagadisan was a renowned social worker. He was awarded with Padmashree in 1957 and international Gandhi award in 1988 for his outstanding contribution in caring for leprosy patients at all India level. With Mahatma Gandhiji's blessings, he started a leprosy home in Mazhavanthangal in South Arcot district. He had taken the initiative to fund the leprosy physiotherapy technician course for 6 months duration in collaboration with CMC hospital, under the leadership of Dr. Paul Brand. He deputed various candidates from different leprosy institutions all over India for the training programme at CMCH.

Accordingly, the training programmes were conducted to treat ulcers in leprosy patients and performing physiotherapy on the deformed hands and feet, and to apply plaster of Paris casts to heal the ulcers. Later, similar programmes were conducted at the leprosy institutes at Karigiri and Chengulpet. This has greatly helped in minimizing the occurrence of ulcers in many leprosy patients and has liberatedthem from their bondage ofb andages to their feet.

Dr. Paul Brand's techniques of healing ulcers spread throughout the world and many countries deputed their candidates to CMC hospital for training. I was made in charge of this leprosy-physiotherapy technicians' training programme under the leadership of Dr. Paul Brand.

This has tremendously helped the patients and it has proven to be a great contribution in the healing of ulcers. Also, his idea of providing micro-cellular rubber footwear (MCR) to leprosy patients for the prevention of ulcers became a boon all over the world.

In those days, patients with ulcers were not wanted in the society. Management of such ulcer treatment made them acceptable. A number of patients got rehabilitated with useful work and became capable of earning their lively hood, instead of begging in the streets or uncared for in the society. The introduction of MCR footwear, for the prevention of ulcers in leprosy patients, not only helped them greatly but also, later on helped diabetic patients who tend to develop ulcers because of their painless feet in advanced cases as well. Currently, it is being largely used by patients who have problems associated with the feet.

When patients came to CMC hospital for treatment, they faced a lot of difficulties in getting accommodation in hotels due to the stigma attached to leprosy. Dr. Paul Brand explained the difficulty of the patients to Prof. T. N. Jagadisan. The latter mobilised some funds through the All India Leprosy Association and bought a house viz. , No. 10 Shanthi illam, near to CMC hospital, for the accommodation of leprosy patients. This house was instrumental for close follow-up of leprosy patients at CMCH and a lot of patients benefitted from it because the accommodation was free.

I was in close contact with Professor T. N. Jagadisan. I used to attend leprosy conferences and present papers on the research work done at CMC hospital, Vellore. Professor T. N. Jagadisan conducted an annual meeting of the Indian Leprosy Relief Association at Chennai and made everybody participate in it.

At one of these meetings, he narrated an incident about Doctor Cochrane. Dr. Cochrane used to treat leprosy patients in Chennai. Among the crowd, he saw a young man standing near him, dressed in a coat, pants, and tie. Dr. Cochrane got angry with him and shouted at him. "Why are you simply standing here? Remove your coat, pant, and tie; then only I can examine you". The young man answered that he was a house surgeon and they had deputedhim to help Dr. Cochrane. That young man was none other than Dr. Rathinavel Subramaniam. Later, he became avery famous doctor in Chennai.

Bombay National All India LEPROSY Workers' CONFERENCE

I attended this conference with Dr. Brand. At the conference, there were a number of exhibition stalls which were installed to depict the work of each leprosy institution. There were some stalls which provided information on recent surgeries of tendon transfers and rehabilitation work for leprosy patients. Dr. Paul Brand stopped at one of the stalls and told me that he has been forgotten by the people as no one mentioned his contribution anywhere in these stalls. I told him, "you are like Thomas Alva Edison who invented electricity. Nobody bothers about his discovery when they switch on the lights. It has become so natural and synonymous and this may be the real success of an individual's efforts and his findings". On hearing this, Dr. Paul Brand laughed and said, "you are intelligent".

Dr. Paul Brand was honoured with Albert Lasker Award in 1960in the USA, which is awarded for outstanding work in the field of rehabilitation medicine. At Vellore CMCH, they had arranged a big meeting in the Scudder Memorial Auditorium to honour him. Dr. Paul Brand, in his acceptance speech, said that he had learnt many things from his patients' history. He also remarked that whenever he performs a new kind of tendon transfer surgery, Mr. Palani would get involved in treating such patients post-operatively. (He also remarked that whenever he does some of the new procedures of tendon surgery, Mr. Palani used to tell me that certain procedure does not allow a tendon to glide freely and gets adherent to the surrounding tissue and creates stiffness in the hand. Following Dr. Paul Brand's speech, many doctors from the auditorium came and congratulated me for my work with him.

Left to Right Dr. S elvapandiyan, Dr. Paul Brand, Mrs. C. K. Job, prof. N. Palani

I was interested in developing devises/splints to correct some of the deformities of the hands and I had mastered the technique of splinting. One of the rich leprosy patients went to Dr. Paul Brand and complained against me, saying that I should take more care of him than the other regular patients and apply splints on him frequently to correct his deformities. Dr. Paul Brand told him that Mr. Palani has more experience in this speciality than him and he is the one who should decide what is good for him.

Dr. Paul Brand chaired a scientific session in a leprosy conference at the national level in Hyderabad in 1962. Dr.

Paul Brand had to present a paper of his research work for which he had prepared slides. The conference hall was fitted with a number of glass windows and the slides could not be presented due to excess lighting. In this situation, I contacted the organisers and I requested them to get some bed sheets and nail them to glass window frames. Dr. Paul Brand was immensely pleased with the arrangements. He presented his paper which was received with a roaring applause. When the time had come for my presentation, I took the opportunity to present my research work on splinting techniques for the deformed hands. My presentation was also received well at the conference.

Dr. Paul Brand personally told me that he was proud of my achievements. It was the month of January; I was wearing a thin khadi dress and was shivering due to the cold weather of Hyderabad. Seeing this, Dr. Paul Brand took me to a shop and got me a sweater which I kept with myself for a number of years. He also told me that he will not be available on the following day for the conference, for the session on rehabilitation. He asked me to show some of the health education posters at the conference which we had prepared at Vellore. I explained the posters to the delegates during the rehabilitation session and they appreciated our work.

The Chairman of the session was late Mrs. Rajkumar Amrit Kaur, the former Health Minister, Government of India. She collected these posters from me and said that she would get them published.

Few months later when I visited some of the hospitals in North India, I saw that those posters had been printed in Regional languages. I was glad of our significant contribution which educated the people at large. These posters could be used to educate people even in remote villages. This kind of work will cut down the health budget of our country. On seeing these posters, my happiness knew no bounds and I felt very happy with our work. I felt that life is full of adventures and heroism.

I used to be invited to the operation theatre by Dr. Paul Brand where I would electrically stimulate the affected nerves and muscles as a part of the research work. Once, an important incident took place when Dr. Herald Gillise, the father of plastic surgery, came to the operation theatre along with Dr. Paul Brand to correct a deformity of the eyelids. The patient was unable to close his eyelids and they would remain widely open all the time. The dust particles would get into his eyes, causing injury. I had to electrically activate the muscle to adjust the tension. With a single touch of an electrode on the motor point, the muscle got activated and Dr. Paul Brand said that I had stimulated the correct point and remarked that I had done an excellent job. As I did this procedure, Dr. Herald Gillise also commended me and asked me to follow up the case post-operatively. The patient fully recovered and left for home happily.

It was indeed very kind of Dr. Paul Brand to have referred my name and a few of my opinions in his operation notes folders. He was also kind enough to refer my name in his autobiography entitled 'Ten fingers for God' and his other book 'Gift of pain'. I was given an opportunity to do a diploma course in physiotherapy and later, a degree course in the same. During this period, I had presented a number of papers at various national and international leprosy conferences. After Dr. Paul Brand had left for America, I used to send him Christmas wishes every year. In his replies, he always encouraged me. He wrote to me saying that, he was very proud of me.

Dr. Paul Brand
1026 California Lane SW
Seattle, WA 98116

3 January 2000

Prof. N. Palani
Vinayaka Mission College of Physiotherapy
Chinna Seeragapadi
Salem 636 308
INDIA

Dear Palani,

It was a great joy to receive your Christmas card and to look through the fine book produced by your College of Physiotherapy. It was good to read your own contribution there and to see your photographs. It would be nice to meet with you and see how much each of us have changed in the intervening years.

Unfortunately your card and the book about the college arrived at my Seattle address while I was actually in India and briefly in Salem itself! If I had received it before I came to India this year I would certainly have tried to contact you in Salem, as I was on my way to the Kolli Mallai to see where I grew up and where my parents worked for so many years.

Do you by any chance ever see Dr. David Elengovan? He has had a clinic in Salem but now has built a medical clinic up on the Kolli Hills in memory of my parents.

It's nice to know you have done so well in your professional life. We are very proud of you. We appreciate that you continue to remember us.

God bless you.

Yours sincerely,

Paul Brand

DEPARTMENT OF HEALTH, EDUCATION, AND WELFARE
PUBLIC HEALTH SERVICE
HEALTH SERVICES ADMINISTRATION
FEDERAL HEALTH PROGRAMS SERVICE

August 5, 1976

TO WHOM IT MAY CONCERN:

I have known Mr. N. Palani for about twenty years during and after his training as a physiotherapist. He has worked under me in the hand research unit at Vellore where he has been responsible for the actual physiotherapy procedures and for the keeping of the records and also for the training of physiotherapy technicians.

Mr. Palani has a deep and thorough understanding of the physiology and mechanisms of the hand and foot and is very thoroughly competent and able to treat patients or to supervise a program or to teach his subject. He is quiet and unassuming and cooperates well with other staff members. I have no hesitation in recommending him for responsible positions as a physiotherapist and especially as one concerned with patients who suffer from leprosy.

Paul W. Brand, F.R.C.S.
Chief, Rehabilitation Branch

Later, Dr. A. J Selvapandian, who had taken up theposition of Dr. Paul Brand, also encouraged me to present and publish papers.

Dr. Paul Brand's Mother

Dr. Brand's mother was a service-minded person. She had been doing missionary work for the tribal people in Kolli hills in South India. She had done commendable work for them, especially in the areas of farming, carpentry, planting trees, animal husbandry, etc.

Having come to know about the good work being done by Dr. Brand's mother at Kolli hills, I went there in 1961 from Vellore to see her. There were no proper roads, to travel. I started climbing the hills one after the other at 10 am and reached the place of Dr. Brand's mother at 4 pm. She was very happy to see me and took me around to show me some of the work which she had done for the tribal people. When she was taking me around, she stopped at one place and said that she lost her husband at a young age, but her strong faith in god keeps her working. People generally expect some appreciation for their good work, but she had no such desire. She continued to do the good work and made many sacrifices for the tribal people.

At present, there are good roads in Kolli hills and the government has taken steps to develop the place.

Mrs. Paul Brand

Mrs. Paul Brand was an eye specialist who worked for leprosy patients. She did extensive research work in the early involvement of the eye in leprosy and evolved methods of treatment to prevent blindness in leprosy patients. She once told me that Dr. Paul Brand works for long hours, continuing till the middle of the night. She wondered if she would lose him because of the strenuous work he undertakes day and night!

One day, when she was sorting Dr. Brand's clothes for laundry, she found a letter in his pocket. It was a letter from the queen of England, inviting him to come and receive the Commander order of the British Empire award.

Dr. Paul Brand had not disclosed this even to his wife and it was a big surprise for her. This incident shows the quantum of dedication Dr. Brand had for his work and that he was not interested in worldly fame. In fact, Dr. Paul Brand's name was on the list of noble prize winners, but before this could be accomplished, he passed away in 2003. In an era when no medical officer was interested in touching leprosypatients' deformed hands. He operated on their hands for the restoration of the function and rehabilitated them.

Shakespeare once said, "None can be called deformed but the Unkind". Dr. Paul Brand used to have lunch with leprosy patients at the rehabilitation center, Navajeeva Nilayam, on Christmas even though he lived nearby. He had a worldwide reputation for his excellent work. Dr. Paul Brand also trained excellent hand surgeons such as Dr. E. P. Fritschi, Dr. Mrs. Karat, and Dr. A. J. Selvapandian and others, who are well-known on international level and have given many publications in leading medical journals. Dr. E. P. Fritschi spent his whole life serving leprosy patients at Vellore and Karigiri and did exemplary work in the field of leprosy.

Dr. Paul Brand promoted team work and encouraged everyone to give the best to the society. He used to arrange a special hand planning clinic every Thursday morning and discuss the problems of hand surgery. Once, about 60 WHO experts had come from all over the world to witness Dr. Paul Brand's great work. In the midst of these experts, I had presented a patient who had been prepared for surgery for both hands. He turned to me and asked whether Dr. Paul Brand could operate on his right hand, but I said that the patient's right hand was swollen and operating on such hands will develop complications, and his left hand is ready for surgery. He burst into laughter and said that I was right. It was great encouragement for me. Though I had several opportunities to serve at the institutions abroad and Indian Government service, I did not quit CMC as I looked for job satisfaction, our own people and I was not after money. Dr. Paul brand had left CMCH and took up a job at Carwille Leprosy Centre, USA in 1965.

After having worked with Dr. Paul Brand for so many years, I consider him as one of the great souls on this earth.

Mahatma Gandhi's interest in Leprosy:

In the context of leprosy, perhaps it may be necessary to mention an incident which took place when Mahatma Gandhi went for his Salt Satyagraha movement in 1930 against the British government at Dandi in Gujarat. Many followers accompanied him in the walk towards Dandi beach, a span of 390 kilometres from their starting point at Sabarmati Ashram in Ahmedabad.

When they gathered for a prayer meeting in the evening, he found that one person was missing from his team. He took a lantern and went out in search of him. At last, he found that this person was sitting on the ground. His foot was bleeding as he had walked a long distance with ulcerated foot and was suffering from leprosy. Gandhiji tore a piece of cloth from his own dress, tied the wound and brought him back to the prayer meeting. The person was made to sit beside Gandhiji in the prayer meeting.

When Gandhi was in his ashram at Wardha, a freedom fighter named Parchure Shastri, a Sanskrit Scholar, suffering from leprosy came to see him. He said that his relatives did not want him and he had nowhere to go. Having seen his pitiful condition, Gandhiji discussed it with the ashram inmates and sought their views regarding whether or not he could admit him in the ashram and care for him. They agreed and Parchure Shastri was given a hut in the ashram. Gandhiji cared for him daily, massaging his limbs. Even today, the hut used by Gandhiji and Parchure Shastri could be seen in Sewagram at Wardha along with a photo showing Gandhiji massaging Parchure Shastri's limbs. Gandhiji's compassion towards the people who were suffering knew no bounds. That is why Albert Einstein remarked about Mahatma Gandhi that "The generation to come will scarcely believe that a man like this with flesh and blood ever lived upon this earth".

Also, Romain Roland called Gandhi another Christ.

Mahatma Gandhi caring a leprosy patient

When Gandhiji was asked to inaugurate a leprosy hospital, Gandhiji declined the offer and said that he can be invited when the hospital gets closed. This shows the vision he had, that the whole population of the country should be healthier. I used to read Mahatma Gandhi's favourite prayer meeting hymns and his writings often inspired me. Some of the favourite hymns/quotes by Mr. M. K Gandhiji which I hold close are given below.

Seven social sins according to Mahatma Gandhi:

Wealth Without Work

Pleasure Without Conscience

Knowledge Without Character

Commerce Without Morality

Science Without Humanity

Religion Without Sacrifice

Politics Without Principle

Vaishnav Janato

- One who is a Vaishnav (one who is a devotee to god)
- Knows the pain of others
- Does good to others, especially to those who are in misery
- Does not let pride overpower his mind
- Tolerates and praises the entire world
- Does not say bad things about anyone
- Keeps his/her words, actions, and thoughts pure
- His mother is blessed
- Sees everything equally, rejects greed and materialism
- Considers someone else's wife/daughter as his mother
- His tongue may get tired, but he will never speak a lie.
- Does not even touch someone else's property
- He does not succumb to worldly attachments
- He has devoted himself to staunch detachment of worldly pleasures
- He has been addicted by the name of Ram

- For whom all the religious sites are in the mind
- Who has no greed and dishonesty
- Who has renounced lust of all types and anger

Mahatma Gandhiji's another favourite reading from the Bible is the 'Sermon on the Mount'.

Sermon on the Mount:

The Be Attitudes

- Blessed *are* the poor in spirit: for theirs is the kingdom of heaven.
- Blessed *are* they that mourn: for they shall be comforted.
- Blessed *are* the meek: for they shall inherit the earth.
- Blessed *are* they which do hunger and thirst after righteousness: for they shall be filled.
- Blessed *are* the merciful: for they shall obtain mercy.
- Blessed *are* the pure in heart: for they shall see God.
- Blessed *are* the peacemakers: for they shall be called the children of God.
- Blessed *are* they who are persecuted for righteousness' sake for theirs is the kingdom of heaven.
- Blessed are ye, when *men* shall revile you, and persecute *you*, and shall say all manner of evil against you falsely, for my sake Rejoice, and be exceedingly glad: for great *is* your reward in heaven: for so persecuted they which were before you.

Father Damien's Sacrifice:

Father Damien was a Catholic missionary who was born in Belgium. In Mulaaki Island, near Hawaai, there was a big leprosy hospital. The leprosy patients at the island suffered greatly due to lack of basic needs. It was decided by the church that one of the Catholic Fathers' should go there and serve them. It was declared that the person who goes there should not return from the sanatorium. This was because in those days, leprosy was considered an incurable disease. After thinking carefully, Father Damien decided to serve at Mulaaki Island and undertook the responsibility of running the institution himself. In the midst of so many difficulties, he started his service there. The patients were devoid of basic facilities like bedding, food, and other medical facilities. He contacted several service organisations for charity and with their help, he did yeomen service for the leprosy patients. He always moved very closely with all the leprosy patients, enquired about their difficulties and tried to solve them.

Father Damien's funeral

One day, steaming hot water spilled on his feet accidentally and caused blisters. He could see the blisters but did not feel the pain at all. On seeing these blisters, he understood that he was also affected by leprosy. In those days, no proper medicines were available for leprosy.

Father Damiensuffereda lot and finally died at the age of 49. Mahatma Gandhi praised Father Damien and said, "such a great sacrificing soul is very rare to see. "

Later on, Catholic leaders in the world together established an organisation called "DAMIEN FOUNDATION" to fund leprosy organisations worldwide. In the year 2009, the Catholic Church praised the services of Father Damien and gave him the title of "Saint Damien". May Father Damien's sacrifice live long! May his name live long!

Dr. K. V. Desikan

In 1958, I was sent on a deputation from CMCH to Gandhi Memorial Leprosy Foundation Centre at Chilakalapali, Andhra Pradesh to train a few leprosy technicians. The institution was run under the leadership of Dr. K. V. Desikan, a renowned pathologist. Dr. Desikan was one of the leading pathologists who had made a big contribution in the field of leprosy. He had received the International Gandhi Award for his outstanding contribution. He also received the Damien Duttan Award for his outstanding work for leprosy patients.

Chilakapalli- a remote Village in Andra Pradesh

Dr. K. V. Desikan receiving Damien Duttan award

Dr. DESIKAN AND THE TEAM

At Chilakapalli, we started doing the village work at 6. 00 AM; conducting survey, educating and treating leprosy patients. We used to walk on uneven grounds and also in some slum areas in the remote villages. The mud used to be very sticky and the footwear used to get lost in that. Many times, it would be difficult to retrieve them back. At times, I used to feel that it would be better to walk barefoot rather than wearing footwear.

On our way, we used to cross small lakes where there used to be lots of water snakes to entertain us. The moment we used to step in the water, the snakes would automatically get in to the water and disappear. It was, indeed, a thrilling experience.

On reaching the village, we used to draw water from a well and clean our feet and then commence our work of treating the patients.

On the first day at Chilakalapalli, when I sat in the clinic, I witnessed seven snakes passing one after another, and I was very frightened. On the following day, when I went out to urinate in the backyard, I realised that there was some twisting movement at the sole of my foot. When I lit the torch, I found out that a snake was lying under my foot and struggling to come out.

One night, there was heavy rain and I could hear the sounds of frogs which were caught by the snakes, crying for help. Being afraid of snakes, I decided not to have dinner that night and stayed back at my quarters. A little later, someone came with an umbrella and a tiffin and knocked at my door. It was none other than Dr. Desikan's wife, Mrs. Kamala Desikan. I was deeply touched by her kindness. She told me that she had come to my place as she was aware that I will not come to their house to eat because of the fear of snakes.

Mrs. Kamala Desikan

Mrs. Kamala Desikan, in her early days, worked at the Gandhi Ashram and served Gandhiji. She joined nursing course and became a nurse and worked at CMCH. She was also a great social worker and encouraged women education. She helped the downtrodden people to move up in their lives. She was a great inspiration to my family. She was the one who encouraged my wife, who had completed only 8th standard at the time of my marriage, to pursue higher education.

She became a close associate of Dr. Sushila Nayar when both of them had served at Gandhi Ashram at Wardha. Dr. Sushila Nayar, health minister of India, came to Vellore for the inauguration of the Spinal CordInjury Centre in 1966. She saw Mrs. Kamala Desikan who was standing at a distance. I remember that Dr. Sushila Nayar left all the dignitaries and came running to her and asked her about her welfare. After leaving CMCH, Mrs. Kamala Desikan established a school in Agra and later served as a secretary at the Mahatma Gandhi Institute of Medical Sciences at Waradha. She had planted 60000 teak wood trees in that Medical College Campus.

International leprosy seminar in Agra

An international leprosy seminar was organized in Agrain 1968 by the Government of India and I was invited to present a paper. On the day of my presentation, I had a temperature of 101degrees Fahrenheit. However, I managed to present my paper and people appreciated my presentation. Dr. Zwicky from Switzerland, who was known to me, asked me to come along with him by plane from Delhi to Chennai. I told him that I had already reserved my train ticket and I would manage to travel by train without difficulty and I thanked him for his kindness.

CALCUTTA CONFERENCE:

I was invited to Chair a Scientific Session at the National Physiotherapy conference in Calcutta. I boarded the train from Chennai, but it suddenly stopped the following morning at 10am at Chitrapur railway station in Odhisha. On enquiry, I was informed that there was a railway strike and it could take at least a minimum of 6 hours to set things right. During this period, I went into the town of Chitrapur and had my hair cut in a salon and bathed in a pool near the railway station. I had my lunch in the town and then resumed my travel. I saw that some of the passengers were climbing on the top of the train due to lack of accommodation in the train. On seeing this, I also climbed to the top of the train and travelled like them for some distance. It was really an enjoyable experience. However, I managed to reach Calcutta on time for the conference and I took the opportunity to visit Birla Planetarium, Calcutta zoo, and Ramakrishna math.

Kumbakonam sacred Heart leprosy hospital:

I was invited by Dr. Zwicky to visit their leprosy hospital in Kumbakonam to help him with their program. I took a few days leave and reached the place. It was a catholic hospital caring for more than 1000 leprosy patients. I told Dr. Zwicky that those patients who were suffering from ulcers and waiting for surgical treatment could stay in the hospital. Rest of them could be discharged so that they can get back to their homes and continue their medical treatment and work productively for their living. Accordingly, a majority of patients were discharged. However, the patients were not happy to leave the place as they got used to the shelter and comfort of the place and being cared for by the Mother Superior and others. However, I advised the patients that they should work hard for their living and they should consider that work is worship and continue their medical treatment without any break.

Dr, A. J. Selvapandiyan

Dr. A. J. Selvapandiyan had become the Head and Professor of the Department of Orthopedics & Leprosy reconstructive surgery when Dr. Paul Brand had left the institution. I had become an expert in applying splints with POP in correcting and releasing of contractures for patients suffering from Leprosy, Rheumatoid arthritis, and other conditions.

Once Dr. A. J. Selvapandiyan asked me ifI would be interested in presenting a paper of mine at the International Leprosy Congress in London in 1968. I told him that it would cost the institution a lot and hence, I could request an American physiotherapist, Mr. Steve Kolumban from Karigiri to present my paper on my behalf as he would be attending this conference anyway. Dr. A. J. Selvapandiyan ultimately agreed to this proposal and it was duly presented by Mr. Steve Kolumban in London on my behalf.

I also travelled with Dr. A. J. S to assist him whenever he went to nearby hospitals to perform surgeries on leprosy patients.

I also used to take a few clinical demonstration classes related to physiotherapy for the medical students and the B. Sc. , Nursing students at CMCH.

Dr. Fritschi

Dr. Fritschi devoted his entire life time for the betterment of leprosy patients. He patiently treated them. Initially, he served at CMC, Vellore, and then in Karigiri. In both the places, he had contributed a lot for the welfare of leprosy patients.

Dr. Mrs. KARAT

Dr. Mrs. Karat was also a close associate of Dr. Paul Brand. She was an expert surgeon. Along with her husband, Dr. Karat, she devoted her whole life for the sake of leprosy patients. Both these doctors are internationally famous for their service at Karigiri and for their multi-drug research work on leprosy. I used to work late in the evening at CMCH. They both would come to me and accompany me for a cup of coffee. I always admired their soft nature. Recently, I had the opportunity of visiting Mrs. Karat at Vellore. I paid my respects to her for the valuable work which they had done for leprosy patients and their multi-drug therapy research work.

Dr. COCHGRANE

I fondly recollect Dr. Cochrane as he made it possible for me to come out of the clutches of leprosy. I was diagnosed with leprosy by him, and he had been instrumental in sending me to Chengulpet for treatment.

Dr. Cochrane had met Mahatma Gandhi at Wardha Ashram and made arrangements for the treatment of leprosy all over our country. Once I met Dr. Cochrane at a seminar in Karigiri and told him that he was the one who diagnosed that I had leprosy and treated me.

He felt immensely happy and told me that I have done well in my life and invited me for dinner at his house.

As a part of his research, Dr. Cochrane used to inject leprosy bacilli in his own body and found that he was not affected by leprosy. So he concluded that leprosy bacilli did not affect people with high resistance power. He also stated that if the treatment was given in the initial stages of leprosy, the disease is completely curable.

Prof. T. N. JAGADISAN

Prof. T. N. Jagadisan along with social workers meeting late President S. Radhakrishnan

Professor T. N. Jagadisan had come in close contact with me and had become a family friend. He used to be interested in my welfare.

Professor T. N. Jagadis an invited me to his institution through Dr. Paul Brand to apply a plaster cast on leprosy patients for ulcers in their feet. I took a cobbler with me to take measurements of their feet. I had applied nearly 15 POP casts with the help of a hurricane lamp, continuing my work even at the nights. When I visited the centre again after 6 weeks and removed all the plaster casts, I found that all the ulcers had healed. Some of these patients had ulcers for more than 10 years and they were suffering from mental agony. On seeing the healed ulcers, the patients were overjoyed and extremely happy. They praised me and said that lord Muruga had come through me to help them.

All the patients were given MCR footwear to prevent recurrence of ulcers.

I visited this institution many times to help the patients there. When I visited the centre recently, I was happy to find that most of the patients were cured and many of them had got rehabilitated.

Adolf Hitler:

Adolf Hitler during the second world war

Concentration camp - War prisoners

During the second world war, Hitler wanted to bring entire Europe under his control and had captured a number of countries viz. , Czechoslovakia, Austria, Belgium, France, Albania, etc. He invaded Great Britain but had strong resistance from its allied powers. Prime Minister Winston Churchill had said, "we shall fight in the beeches, we shall fight on the land, we shall fight in the fields and in the streets, we shall fight in the huts, we shall never surrender".

When Hitler captured war prisoners, he arrested them and kept them in Nazi concentration camps. He treated them very cruelly and the condition of these prisoners was miserable. He in humanly accommodated hundreds of Jews in a single room and through pipes, passed cyanide gas inside these rooms, thus killing a number of Jews with a single stroke. While all this was happing on one side of the world, Group Captain Cheshire, after seeing the calamities of the bombing of Nagasaki, took up humanitarian work. The destruction that the war had created and the sufferings that people underwent changed his mind and he decided to quit the army and started serving humanity.

Disaster of atom bomb-Nagasaki - JAPAN

Among the honours that Cheshire received as a pilot, the Victoria Cross is the highest and most prestigious award for gallantry in the face of the enemy that can be awarded to British and Commonwealth forces.

Author with the group captain Cheshire

He was the youngest Group Captain in the RAF and one of the most highly decorated pilots of the War but after serving as the British observer on the Nagasaki nuclear attack, he resigned from the Air Force. Later on, he established a hospice which grew into the charity named Leonard Cheshire Disability Homes.

After seeing the calamities of the war, he decided to serve the elderly all over the world. I had come in contact with him on few occasions when he was at Vellore, CMCH. I helped him in the developmental work of Cheshire Home at Katpadi, Vellore. I was also an executive member of the Cheshire home at Katpadi. I remember that Baron Cheshire sometimes used to travel on a bicycle in Vellore like any other common man. He became known for his work in conflict resolution; he was honoured as Baron Cheshire in 1991 for the recognition of his charitable work.

Baron Cheshire consulted me for making a film on Cheshire Home at Katpadi. For the making of the film, we went to a small lake near Chittoor and shot there. He also asked me to take a class for the students. He even wrote a letter to me, stating that my part of taking the class had come out very well and it was telecasted on Canadian television. I fondly remember that every New Year, I used to receive a greeting card from Group Captain Cheshire.

Dr. Sushila Nayar:

Dr. Sushila Nayar was the former Health Minister, Government of India, and also the Chairman of the Mahatma Gandhi Institute of Medical Sciences at Wardha.

I attended the National Leprosy Conference at Wardha in 1973 where she addressed the meeting and mentioned her involvement in a number of health programmes and her achievements.

When she stepped off the dais, I met her and told her that her real work was during the freedom struggle and that she is presently enjoying the fruits of her labour. She was very surprised by my remarks and she invited me for lunch to which I agreed. When the lunch break was announced at the conference hall, I was accompanied by my friends to the conference dining hall. Dr. Sushila Nayar was standing at the entrance and asked me why I was not attending the lunch programme at her residence. I felt ashamed and apologised for my mistake, then I accompanied her.

Mahatma Gandhi peace mission-Navakali

On our way, she narrated some of the incidences she experienced while she was working with Mahatma Gandhi. She narrated an incident when Gandhiji had asked his followers to go on a peace mission to Nowakali, walking a great distance. One of the followers asked Gandhiji what reward they would get for their struggles. Gandhi replied that death will be the reward and giving up one's life for a noble cause like this would be the greatest service to humanity.

During the journey, they stayed in a bungalow for a short period of time. Suddenly, a mob started throwing stones at the glass windows of the bungalow and it broke. Mahatma said that he would happily embrace death among his own people if it happens so. He came out of the bungalow and people started shouting at him, stating that he is showing partiality towards the Muslim community. He addressed the gathering and convinced them about the importance of the peace mission.

In the end, people started shedding tears. This was the greatness of Mahatma Gandhi.

Dr. Sushila Nayar had requested me to find some doctors to work for her institution, but she laid down a condition that those who would work with her should be honest, vegetarians, non-alcoholics and non-smokers. I told her that it will be difficult to find such doctors. She replied that if they join her institution, they will become more stable and will work for a noble cause and they will not be yielded to the temptations.

Dr. Marry Verghese:

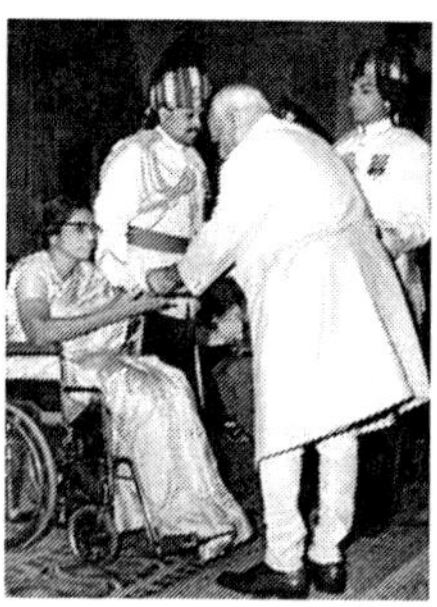

Dr. Mary Verghese receiving Padmasree award

Dr. Marry Verghese was one of the outstanding doctors in the field of rehabilitation for the disabled. While she was working as a house surgeon at CMCH, Vellore, she went for a picnic with her friends and she met with an accident which caused injury to the spinal cord. Both her legs got paralyzed and she was unable to walk. Dr. Paul Brand was interested in her rehabilitation and taught her how to perform surgery while sitting in a wheel chair. Later on, she became an expert surgeon. She used to commute in a wheel chair to get to her quarters in the same campus. At times, when needed, I used to push the wheel chair to her quarters.

Miss. Dorathy (Dorothy) Clarke Wilson, a famous writer, and author, had written to me asking whether I could contribute in writing about Dr. Marry Verghese as she wanted to publish a book on her name. As requested, I helped Miss. Dorathy Clarke Wilson. When the book was published, it had a very wide circulation all over the world. It wasabout the great work that Dr. Marry Verghese had done in the field of rehabilitation, inspite of her disability. Dorathy Clarke Wilson was kind enough to include my name in the list of contributing authors of the book. Subsequently, Dr. Marry Verghese established a spinal cord injury centre at Vellore CMCH, which has become a globally recognized centre for spinal cord injury patients.

A four limbs amputee:

We had a patient with four limb amputations. Both his lower limbs above the knee and both the upper limbs above the elbow had been amputated. He had to be carried like a baby to the hospital. After thorough assessment, doctors referred this patient to various disciplines such as physiotherapy, occupational therapy, artificial limb making centre and to a social worker. All the teams worked on this patient and vigorous physiotherapy was given to him. The unaffected muscles of his limbs were strengthened so that he could walk and carry out his day to day activities by himself using his own artificial limbs.

He was given rigorous training and artificial lower limbs were given to him. He started walking in parallel bar. Consequently, he started walking independently with artificial limbs.

Similarly, for the upper limbs, an artificial limb was fitted and he was able to eat his food, brush his teeth, comb his hair and do other functional activities.

At the spinal cord injury centre, I was impressed with one young physiotherapist. She used to work really hard with these patients; strengthening their muscles without wasting her time. I asked her why she dedicated to those patients. She told me that she wanted to give the best of her youth by serving these patients through which she can serve god. I marveled at her attitude and sympathy shown by her towards the patients and others.

SHRIBABA AMTE

Shri Baba Amte with his admirers

Shri Baba Amte was a great social worker who did pioneering work in improving the livelihood of disabled people. He is the recipient of Magsaysay Award for his outstanding contribution towards disabled people. Shri Baba Amte often used to say, "Charity destroys but work builds". He himself had disabilities due to spinal cord problems. Inspite of being disabled, he did pioneering work in the field of rehabilitation of leprosy patients and for other disabled patients.

Shri Baba Amte was running rehabilitation centre for the disabled, especially for leprosy patients and also for other disabilities caused due to poliomyelitis, road accidents, blindness, etc. Dr. Paul Brand had suggested that the Vellore team should conduct a research program at Baba Amte's Rehabilitation centre in Warora near Nagpur.

The team was headed by Dr. A. J. Selva Pandian along with a physiotherapist, an occupational therapist, a social worker, and a bio-statistician with a clinical assistant. Our task was to assess the deformities of leprosy patients, their absence of pain sensation, muscle power, etc. in detail. We also studied the frequency of ulcers in patients doing agricultural work. The centre was also equipped with other rehabilitation programmes such as agriculture, weaving, tin can projects, tailoring, carpentry, greeting card making, etc. When our team arrived at the rehabilitation centre, we were warmly welcomed by Baba Amte and his wife.

Leprosy patients at work at Baba Amte's rehabilitation centre

We started assessing leprosy patients for their disabilities and loss of pain sensation, mainly in hands and feet. The most painful thing about leprosy is the lack of sense of pain. Patients without pain sensation in their hands can put their hands inside fire and not complain of pain. If there is no pain sensation in their feet, then, while walking barefoot, thorns or broken glass pieces may get inside their feet and cause ulcers and infection. Though these patients may not suffer from active leprosy, except for the loss of sensation of pain, they get injured this way.

While assessing the patients, I observed that the female farmers were wearing gold bangles and chains. It was a big surprise for us to see them this way. I asked them how it was possible for them to buy these gold ornaments.

They replied that they all work hard in the field without wasting time and buy gold ornaments with the money they earn. We also saw huge halls filled with dhal in gunny bags. Similarly, we also found large quantities of wheat products were also put in their storage. These commodities were sold in the public market. I saw a leprosy patient who had deformities in both hands and feet and he was carrying a small drum and a stick. Upon enquiry, he said that he is going to the wheat field to drive the parrots away by beating the drums to prevent the crops from getting damaged. Few of them had deformities and they were given suitable jobs according to their disability. For example, if there are no fingers in the hand a broom can be tied on to the forearm so that they can sweep the floor without any difficulty. I saw a few blind patients who were climbing the trees and playing around. And some of the blind patients were given work to remove the dried seeds from the corns.

I also saw a number of jeeps coming to this centre one after another. I enquired one of the workers why so many jeeps were coming to this place. He said that a Minister has come to see Baba Amte for a discussion on rehabilitation programmes. He also said that Baba Amte will not go and see the Minister. If the Minister is interested in any information, then he should come to see him directly.

Baba Amte took our team to his area in Somnath forest and gave us lodgings in their building. He said that the rehabilitation work is being done for the tribal people.
When night had crept in, he casually mentioned that tigers may roam around the place. We got frightened and we all bolted the doors and windows carefully.

What I observed was that none of the patients was lazy and everybody was put into some productive work or other, in line with their disability, so that the patients were useful to the society at large and they could maintain their self-esteem and have a decent living.

Few months later, we had to assess the disabilities of leprosy patients and send a report to the USA for further research. In this regard, Dr. A. J Selvapandian sent a letter to Baba Amte for permission to visit their centre and do our assessment. Sri Baba Amte replied to this letter stating that it will not be possible to entertain the team because he had already arranged a youth camp at his centre. As we had to send the report to USA immediately, Dr. A. J. Selvapandian asked me to meet Baba Amte personally and explain our difficulties and to convince him for the necessary permission. I boarded the train and left for Baba Amte's place near Nagpur. I met Baba Amte and explained to him about our immediate need to assess the leprosy patients in order to prepare our report.

He said that the place will be fully occupied and it will not be possible for him to provide accommodation for us. I said that we do not require any special accommodation and that we could even sleep on the floor and look at the sky, thinking of the almighty. After hearing these words from me, he gave the permission. Few days later, the entire team from Vellore arrived, including a European lady, an occupational therapist who had also come to do the assessment. Baba Amtewas initially upset, but he made the necessary arrangements. Finally, the rooms were allotted and we continued to do our assessment. All this happened during the summer in the central part of India which is very hot, and temperatures soar upto 117 degree Fahrenheit.

I visited a leprosy center, Maharogi Seva Samithi, in Wardhain which Mahatma Gandhi was interested. I went and stayed there for a few days in1970 and offered technical assistance

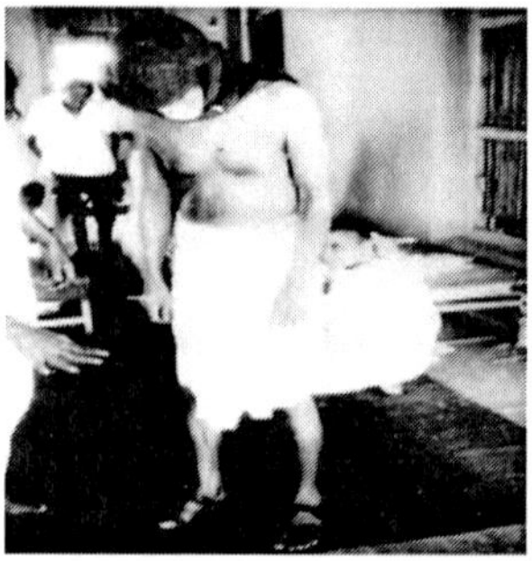

Authour meeting shri. Vinoba bhave

to the workers especially in applying plaster cast to treat ulcer and provide them with MCR foot wear to prevent its recurrence. The Medical superintendent, Dr. R. S. Sharma was very interested in this programme and he took me to Shri Vinoba Bhave. He was fighting along with Mahatma Gandhi and was staying at Pavanar ashram.

Acharya Vinoba Bhave was a freedom fighter and a spiritual leader. He was deeply concerned about the deprived masses. Vinoba Bhave had once said, "All revolutions are spiritual at the source. All my activities have the sole purpose of achieving a union of hearts. " In 1958, Vinoba was the first recipient of the international Ramon Magsaysay Award for Community Leadership. He was also conferred with Bharat Ratna posthumously in 1983, which is India's highest civilian award.

Though Shri. Vinoba Bhave had done commendable work for freedom struggle and was the leader of Bhoodan movement, collecting lands from the rich people and offering them to the poor, he was never interested in holding any high position, inspite of the various offers which had come to him. He led a saintly life in his old age. The Medical superintendent introduced me to Shri

Shri. Vinobha bhave-Bhoodhan movement

Vinoba Bhave. He was pleased with my assistance offered to their centre.

I told him that along with Bhoodan movement, he should also help in the rehabilitation work of leprosy patients. He was so pleased in meeting me that he gave me a book on Bhagavath Gita which was written by him and he also signed the book in Tamil. I had met him once again after 2 years and paid my respects to him.

BHAGAVAD GITA

The Bhagavad Gita (Song of God) is the essence of the Vedas and Upanishads. It is a universal scripture applicable to people of all temperaments, for all times. It is a book with sublime thoughts and practical instructions on Yoga, Devotion, and Vedanta. Gandhiji used to remark that whenever he gets into a difficult situation in life, he finds solace in mother Gita. The Bhagavad Gita has influenced many great thinkers over the years and was a great inspiration in my life. The essence of Bhagavad Gita which impressed me the most is given below:

Below is the brief essence of the philosophy of Bhagavad Gita. Teachings of Bhagavad-Gita were given by Lord Krishna, the God Himself, to his disciple, Arjuna on the battlefield of Kurukshetra in Haryana, India. These teachings were given more than 5000 years ago but these are still relevant today in our lives.

BHAGAVAD GITA SUMMARY (in English)

Whatever happened in the past, it happened for good; whatever is happening, is happening for good;

Whatever shall happen in the future shall happen for good only.

Do not weep for the past; do not worry for the future, concentrate on your present life.

What did you bring at the time of birth that you have lost?

What did you produce which is destroyed?

You didn't bring anything when you were born.

Whatever you have, you have received it from the God only while on this earth.

Whatever you will give, you will give it to God.

Everyone came in this world empty handed and shall go the same way. Everything belongs to God only.

Whatever belongs to you today, belonged to someone else earlier and shall belong to someone else in future. Change is the law of the universe.

You are an indestructible soul and not a body. Body is composed of five elements - Earth, Fire, Water, Air, and Sky; one day body shall perish with these elements.

Soul lives forever even after death as soul is never born and never dies. So why do you worry unnecessarily? What are you afraid of? Who can kill you?

Devote yourself to the Almighty only. One who takes the support of God, always gains freedom from fear, worry, and despair.

My Family

I got married in the year 1963. Before my marriage, I had laid down a condition that I will not accept any dowry and the marriage should be conducted in a temple without spending too much. Ms. Dhanalakshmi was educated only up to 8th standard and I took an assurance from her that she had to study further after our marriage.

A day before my wedding, I went to the temple and found that the place was unclean and full of leaves. I took a broom and swept the place around. On the day of my wedding, all the relatives and friends had come and they appreciated the simple way in which the wedding ceremony was conducted.

Few months later, our family went for a picnic and I got into a swimming pool. I was able to swim in shallow water and I was quite happy. Little later, I went into the deep water and I could not succeed in coming out of the swimming pool and I was showing my hands for someone to rescue me. People around the place thought that I was simply joking, but one of them felt that I needed help. I almost thought that was the end of my life. That person got into the swimming pool and caught me by my hair and brought me out and placed me on the floor, and thus, I was rescued. I thought that god wanted me to live for some more time for some purpose. Witnessing this event, my wife was very much frightened.

I was drawing a salary of Rs. 100/month, I paid Rs. 25/month for her tuition fees and I was able to manage with less than Rs. 75 and run the family economically. When she was about to write her SSL Cexam, she was a bit nervous to write the exam as she was pregnant. I took her to the CMC hospital and the gynecologist had said that it will take another 2 week time, and thus she can write the exams without fear. Accordingly, she wrote her exams and passed it with flying colours.

She delivered a baby girl and we named her Vasughi. My wife passed her SSLC and wanted to pursue her studies further. When Vasughi was one-year old, my wife got admission in a teachers' training program for a duration of two years. The training center was about 40 km away from Vellore town, with a compulsory residenceship course. My younger sister assured me that she will take care of the child so that my wife can pursue the course. She joined the course and used to come and visit the family every month. On completion of teachers' training programme, she got a job as a secondary grade teacher in Vellore municipality. She studied further by postal correspondence and passed MA and then B. Ed. I suggested to my wife that she need not pursue Ph. D or other higher education, since it may involve transfer to some other distant places which will affect the smooth running of our family and care of the children. She agreed to do so.

We brought our second child into the world after five years of our marriage and named her Kalaivani. I used to be very involved with the work in the hospital; treating patients and often came home late in the evening.

I used to get a very meagre salary at CMC hospital in those days and my wife was a secondary grade school teacher. It used to be difficult to run the family and educate the children. However, our needs were less and we led a simple life, so we managed without much difficulty.

My Mother

Though my mother had mental illness, she did not give any problem to the people around her. She was very co-operative and helpful to the family. She used to sing very well. When my father passed away, she was not aware of his death and took a hand fan to fan him. My father had taken immense care of her. I used to wash her clothes and helped her by all means. My wife, Dhanalkshmi, was also very affectionate towards her and used to help her in all her daily chores and feed her timely. My sisters, Pappi, and Kantha, lived in the same street. They used to be very loving to our family and assisted us intaking care of my mother and in bringing up our children as we both used to go to work.

Dr. C. K. Job:

Dr. C. K. Job was a renowned pathologist in leprosy work and he was also the principal of the Christian Medical College, Vellore. He was interested in my welfare and cared for me. When I had invited his family for dinner at my residence, he accepted it and came to my house. He enquired about our children's education. I said that I will educate them to some degree course. On seeing the grades of my children, he said that they were scoring such high marks and advised me to enrol them in some professional course such as medicine or engineering. His words inspired me and encouraged me greatly. I got both my daughters into professional education which was not a common thing in those days.

Women did not get professional education at par with men in those days. It was a general thinking that if you educate a girl, then it may attract more dowry if she is more educated than her future husband. Hence, people around me dissuaded me from putting my daughters in professional courses, saying that I will encounter unnecessary trouble later. However, I strongly believed that education was the only means of upliftment in life and my children should get the best education possible. Right from their early days, I used to send them to the best convent schools at Vellore and also got them higher professional education at good colleges, though it was beyond my means. However, we managed by curtailing other expenditure and living a very simple life.

My eldest daughter Vasughi:

My eldest daughter Vasughi had always been good at studies. I was determined to give her the best possible professional education. Accordingly, she got admission in College of Engineering, Guindy on merit basis. After that, she was selected as an engineer at NLC India Limited (NLCIL), Government of India, a public sector undertaking. She worked hard and got a number of promotions and is now working as the Deputy General Manager. She is married to an engineer, Mr. Muralibabu, who also worked and retired as a Chief General Manager in the same company. He is a dynamic, straight forward and hard working person. He is an expert in the field of lubrication of specialized mining equipment. Their daughter, M. V. Brindha, is equally brilliant and has received a gold medal in her engineering course. She is further pursuing higher education. Her husband, Mr. Munireddy, is a brilliant young man and both of them are working for the Government of India. I am also blessed with a great grand daughter, Nivedita.

Dr. Kalaivani

Dr. Kalaivani is my second daughter. While she was studying in the9th standard, she didn't score good marks in her exams. She was very playful and did not listen to our advice to study well.

Therefore, I met the Mother superior of the school and requested her to advice my daughter to study well. Her class teacher warned her in the middle of the class. My daughter was very upset and came crying to me. But gradually, she showed improvement at her studies. When she was studying in 10th standard, I saw her getting full marks in Chemistry. I thought that if she could get full marks in one subject, why not in other subjects too? Therefore, I encouraged her to study well and arranged extra classes for her. She worked hard in her plus 2 exams and scored high marks. She got admission in one of the most prestigious medical colleges in Chennai-Kilpaulk Govt Medical College(KMC) on merit basis. She passed her MBBS and she pursued PG studies in Obstetrician and Gynaecology at CMC Hospital and became the recipient of a gold medal in her field in 1996.

In those days, it was customary to perform arranged marriages wherein we had to look out for suitable grooms. So, I was looking for a suitable groom for Kalaivani. A boy's family came to my house for an alliance with my daughter. He said that there was no parking place in our house. On hearing this, I dropped that alliance. The second person who had come for an alliance stated that their son is studying P. G. Medical -MRCP in England. He suggested that my daughter should stop her PG studies and get married at an early date. Then I told them that their son can stop his studies in England and they can then arrange for the marriage. After listening to my words, the family left the place. When the 3rd alliance came, I went into their town and enquired about the boy's conduct and people there told me that he was an alcoholic and therefore, I dropped that alliance too.

When the 4th alliance viz. , Dr. Kulothunga Sozhan had come from Chengum, a small town in Tiruvanamalai district, he told me that he will not interfere with my daughter's studies and he would like to get married to her. They got married and they have a small nursing home, consisting of 10 beds, an operation theatre, an ultra sound scanning machine, Echo Cardiogram, and a pharmacy. They work for the people around the villages. Dr. Kulothunga Sozhan is also one of the Board of Directors of the Vivekananda Educational Trust which runs the Vivekananda Matriculation Higher Secondary school in Chengum. He is so dedicated to the school children that he personally handles physics and zoology classes forthe12th standard students. They are happy with 2 children. Her daughter, Ilakia, is studying MBBS now and her son, Mukilan, has passed 12thstandard and he will be pursuing further studies.

My Relatives

My elder sister Mrs. Pappi and younger sister, Mrs. Kantha lived near our ancestral house. They were very affectionate towards me and cared for my two children as my wife was working as a teacher in a school. My younger sister, Kantha and her husband, Arunachalam, had no children of their own and cared for my two kids as theirs. Without their support, it would have been very difficult for my wife to pursue higher education. Whenever our kids fell sick, I remember my uncle, Arunchalam, would hold the kids in his arms and walk throughout the night without sleep. I am witnessing that such sort of selfless love and affection is becoming a rare commodity these days.

My elder sister always was a source of moral support for me. I used to visit my sister's place everyday after work and supervise her children who were studying at school. My elder sister's children, Sridhar, Uma Shankar, Usha, Geetha, and Sekar were fond of me and my family. The moment I would arrive, I could see them with books in their hands. Perhaps their mother had threatened them by using my name.

I used to take ourphysiotherapy students to a nearby forest called Amirthi or to a dam called Sathanoor, almost every year for picnic. My family, my children, and my relatives' kids also used join these picnics. There was a small stream in the forest and a mini zoo where the children and the students used to play the whole day and enjoy themselves. I remember those days when my sister used to prepare and pack huge quantities of lemon rice, curd rice, and poha which everybody used to relish so much, as her cooking used to be very tasty.

My younger sister Parvathi had got married in the nearby village and though she did not live with us, she has been very affectionate towards my family and I. When my wife had total knee replacement of her both knees, she came and helped her for nearly two months which is a rare act of kindness.

Whenever my family visited our relatives in Chennai, the moment we'd reach the railway station, we used to visit the old zoo near moor market, putting all our luggage in the clock room. We also went to the Marina beach in the evening and had a good time playing in the water and later to the Parthasarathy temple to worship.

Once when my family went to Madurai temple, my second daughter, Kalaivani got lost in the huge temple. We thoroughly searched for her and at last, we found her near the goddess statue and the priest was enquiring about her. After seeing us, she was very happy and joined the group. Whenever I go to my relatives' house, I used to tell my children to wake up early in the morning and finish their daily routine, so that we would not cause inconvenience to others during our stay.

Whenever the children fell sick with fever or cold, it was my younger sister, Kantha who would immediately take them to CMCH for treatment as my wife had to go to school. My cousin brother, Shri Kadirkaman, was a psychologist at CMCH Vellore and later on joined government service and built up a good reputation for his work. He was very close to me and my family and was more of my own brother than my cousin.

All my other cousins, Dr. Jaganathan, Dr. Manonmani, Vanaja, Dhaksnamoorthy, Murugesan, Saravanan, are also very close to us. Dr. Jaganathan, who retired as Director of Medical Services of Tamil Nadu was a very honest officer.

Mr. Chandrasekaran is our relative who used to be engaged in social services. Whenever there is an unclaimed body after death nearby, he even travels in the middle of the night and collects the eyes for restoration of sight of some blind person. The dead body was collected and given to medical colleges. Also, he used to collect the excess food from hotels, functions, and other marriages and gave it to orphanages.

On every Independence Day or Republic Day, I used to celebrate it in our street with photos of national leaders, inorder to develop patriotism in the minds of the children living nearby. I also used to ask the school going children to speak about independence. One day, I found that posters were displayed in Vellore that Mr. D. Moorthy, my relative who held the post of professor in Aligarh Muslim University will be speaking in a public meeting.

On enquiring Mr. Moorthy on how come he had become a prominent speaker, he told me that in his school days, he used to participate in the Independence Day celebrations in our street which gave him the inspiration in public speaking.

Another cousin of mine, Mr. Dhakshnamoorthy, was an excellent football player at the state level and later became a coach at the state level. While talking to him, he remarked that he used to watch me play football which had inspired him.

I felt very happy over these replies from Dr. D. Moorthy and Mr. Dhakshinamoorthy.

My Patients:

I had a patient who was working as a Deputy Collector and he was suffering from leprosy. He had deformed hands and feet. He was introduced to me by my close relative, Mr. P. T. Sambandan, who was also a Deputy Collector in the same district. Furthermore, this patient was neglected by his family members. He had lost faith in living. He had even made an attempt to commit suicide. When he had come to me, I counseled him and treated his hands so as to make his hand more useful. I had also taken him to a leprosy home and showed him how they have been rehabilitated and became useful members of the society. Having been successfully treated and encouraged, he joined Government services again. He further got promotions and started to support his family members once again.

I had a female attender who had been working with me at Vinayaga missions, Salem. Her husband beat her and their children frequently after consuming alcohol and had developed all sort of bad habits. I told her to learn typing and financially helped her for the typewriting course. She passed her higher grade in typing and gradually learnt to operate a computer. Presently she is working in an office and uses computer.

A leprosy patient aged 18, suddenly developed foot drop and was unable to walk properly. She was walking with a limp. Her parents had already arranged a marriage for her, but the marriage was stopped eventually because of her disability. We had treated this patient with a plaster of Paris cast and asked her to report to us after four weeks. When the plaster was removed, it was a great surprise for her to see her foot functioning normally again. The marriage which was cancelled was rearranged and she started living a happy married life.

A female patient, aged 10, came with both hands deformed and was unable to grasp a tumbler or pick-up a coin or a pen from the table. Her brother, who had accompanied her, said that they hail from a poor family and were worried about the future of his sister.

I said that it is possible to correct her deformed hands through surgery and physiotherapy. They were also worried about the future prospects of her marriage. We treated her successfully and I suggested him to educate her to the maximum level possible.

15 years later, her brother came to my residence and on seeing me, started crying. I asked him whether his sister was facing any problem. He said, "according to your advice, I

had educated her upto M. A. , and B. Ed. , She got a job as a lecturer in a college". She also developed friendship with a professor who was working in the same college. They got married. However, as her husband belonged to a different caste, their tradition did not accept them in their family and they abandoned her. Hearing this, I told him that tradition and castism die hard and he should not abandon his sister. You have to accept her in your family since she was able to get a good job and maintain herself with respect and dignity in her life in spite of her adversities.

We had a patient in no. 10 Shanthi illam, near CMCH, who had deformities in both the hands. One day, he wanted to travel to his native place by bus and requested me to help him to the bus as he had deformities. I helped him to get into the bus. However, the conductor refused to allow the leprosy patient to travel in the bus. I told the conductor that the patient holds a negative certificate and he is not infectious to others and hence he can be allowed to travel in the bus. However, the conductor strongly refused and asked the patient to get out of the bus. I said that I will not allow the bus to proceed further and said that I will put my head in front of wheel of the bus and got into an argument. But the patient felt a bit embarrassed and requested me not to pursue the matter and said that he will travel by train at a later date.

Spinal cord injury patients:

I found from the history of the patients that they invariably fall from height of a tree and land on their buttocks. When there is a severance of the spinal cord, invariably they land up with paralysis of both lower limbs and sometimes of all the four limbs. With no movement in their limbs, the patient finally ceases to move.

Mother Teresa caring for the under privileged

The bladder and bowel controls can also be lost in such patients. The life of these patients is quite miserable as they are unable to walk. Usually, they are given supportive calipers and are made to walk with help of crutches. For those who are severely disabled, they will have to resort to wheel chair activity only. They also need supportive splints which are quiet expensive. I, therefore, planned to make splints with bamboo support. I also made parallel bars with bamboos and also a walker and a few other splints for the disabled patients. These splints are inexpensive and can be made by locally available materials. Patients who have lower limbs paralyses and functioning upper limbs can be exercised for crutch walking. The treatment is incomplete until and unless they are able to earn their livelihood. Simple jobs like tailoring or owning a petty shop, typing, are some of the useful jobs that they could be deployed in to earn their livelihood.

I attended an international leprosy conference during 1984 in New Delhi and emphasized about the less expensive splints made out of bamboo for the upper and lower limb. I listened

The author with delegates meeting the then prime minister Mrs Indira Gandhi at delhi

to Mother Theresa's address at the inaugural function at Vigyan Bhavan, New Delhi. I also took the opportunity of meeting the then Prime Minister, Indira Gandhi at her residence.

Testing the effect of neem oil on rats

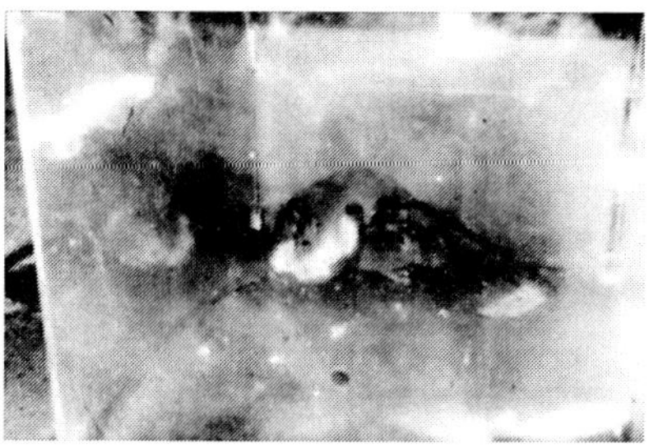

Testing the effect of neem oil

Asleprosy patients cannot feel pain, there are ample chances for ants, cockroaches, and rats to bite their legs and cause wounds. However, when neem oil is applied on the feet and the patient is made to stand even on an anthill, the ants kept away from the feet. I arranged a rattrap in which we kept two pieces of coconut, one piece without neem oil and the other piece smeared with it. The rats which entered the trap ate the plain coconut piece only and avoided the other piece smeared with neem oil.

I took photographs of all the experiments I had undertaken, and in the year 1973, I explained these facts with the help of slides at the All India Leprosy Conference at Wardha. As a result, a number of leprosy patients benefitted and were able to escape from insect bites by applying simple neem oil on their feet. This method is very effective as a number of patients could apply neem oil which is relatively cheaper and thus keep away from rat bites.

It was also found that applying neem oil to the exposed area of the body prevents muscuto bites and thus prevents developing muscuto related diseases . It also prevents drying of the skin . Of all the above methods destroying the muscuto are paramount importance as a preventive method.

I was the head of the Physiotherapy education programme at CMCH, Vellore. I maintained high quality of education and the Vellore students always topped the list in the MGR medical University. Whenever our physiotherapy graduates applied for jobs in India and abroad, they invariably got it without any problem.

I am extremely proud to say that many of our students have done very well in their professions in our country and abroad. To mention a few, a student of mine called Thomas Mathew had gone to USA and established almost 5 physiotherapy clinics at various places. He did a Masters degree in Orthopaedics and Sports medicine. He also worked as the Director of a Rehabilitation centre in USA. But at one stage, he felt that he should come back to India. As wished, he came back and started a home for disabled children in Vellore. Now, along with Mr. Ruby Rathinakumar, he is giving yeoman service to differently-abled children.

During his student days, he used to be interested in extra-curricular activities and visit the spinal cord injury centre at CMCH, along with other students, to clear the bushes in the vicinity of the building. This cleaning used to be a regular programme every month and all the students enjoyed doing this work in the Gandhian way. Along with our students, Dr.

Suranjan Bhatacharjee (former Director of CMCH) and I used to clean the place too.

One more student of mine, Mr. Manickam, serves leprosy patients at the Saint Mary's Leprosy Hospital in Salem. He goes to remote villages to treat them. He mobilises funds from charitable organisations and provides livelihood to rehabilitate leprosy patients by giving them cows and sheep so that through cattle rearing those patients can make a living and stand on their feet without expecting anybody's help. He also takes the students to the villages to create awareness about leprosy.

My retirement at CMCH:

During the year 1996, when I was about to retire from CMCH, I was offered a number of jobs, including to work as a Principal in various physiotherapy colleges in Tamil Nadu. The Chairman of one of the physiotherapy colleges offered me a job stating that I can fix the salary for myself and not by their institution. However, the Chairman of Vinayaga Missions rang up to me and asked me to assume the post of the principal of their physiotherapy college at the earliest. I had preferred and joined Vinayaga missions, as it was attached to a medical college, having facilities to teach anatomy, physiology and various subjects in addition to treatment of patients through physiotherapy.

Chairman, Vinayaga missions, Salem:

The Chairman of Vinayaga missions, Dr. Shanmuga Sundaram, had a humble beginning and started this institution with the blessings of the great Tamil scholar, Thirumuruga Girupananda Varrior. With the support of Swamy Kirupananda Varrior, he had started a small Pharmacy college. Due to his strenuous hard work and vision, he expanded the institution on a wider scale. He went on to add a Nursing college, a Physiotherapy college, an Engineering college and Medical college in that list. More than 20,000 students benefitted every year from these institutions.

Currently, the Vinayaga Missions institution has around thirty colleges and employs thousands of people. Students from in and around India study in these colleges. Dr. Shanmuga Sundaram has also built a massive temple near the university which has become a favourite place for pilgrims all over Tamil Nadu and India.

His two sons Dr. Sharavanan, Dr. Ganesan and the other Directors, work hard for the growth of these institutions.

When I was offered a quarter to stay inside the college campus, I found that the land was barren and devoid of any plants. As soon as I occupied the quarters, I planted a drumstick plant and started watering it. I was surprised to see it growing very fast. So, I planted banana saplings which also grew rapidly. I bought around 20 mango saplings and distributed them to my neighbours there. Seeing this, many of my neighbours took interest in gardening and planted more saplings in their gardens. All these plants grew very well and soon, the barren land started to look bright and green. I was very happy to see that so much of land can be used productively even with little effort.

When I was to retire from Vinagayaga Missions in 2004, the Chairman requested me to continue my services and upgraded my position as the Director of the Physiotherapy College. I received a letter from the Chairman as follows:

THIRUMURUGA KIRUPANANDA VARIYAR
THAVATHIRU SUNDARA SWAMIGAL
MEDICAL EDUCATIONAL AND CHARITABLE TRUST

Administrative Office : Sankari Main Road, Ariyanoor, Salem-636 308. Tamilnadu, India.
Phone : 0427-2477316/317/594/598 Fax : 0427-2477303 E-mail : vmtrust@vinayakamission.com Web : www.vinayakamission.com

Ref :

Date : 19 .04.2004

OFFICE ORDER

Vinayaka Mission's Management is very happy and pleased towards excellent service put in by you as Principal of Vinayaka Mission's College of Physiotherapy, Salem.

Considering your outstanding performance, the Vinayaka Mission's management appoint you as Director and hereby informed you to assume the office of the Director,VM College of physiotherapy from the F/N of 19.04.2004.

With Best Regards.

CHAIRMAN

To,

Prof.N.Palani
Principal,
Vinayaka Mission's College of Physiotherapy,
Salem – 636 308.

B.P.T students – vinayaka missions – salem

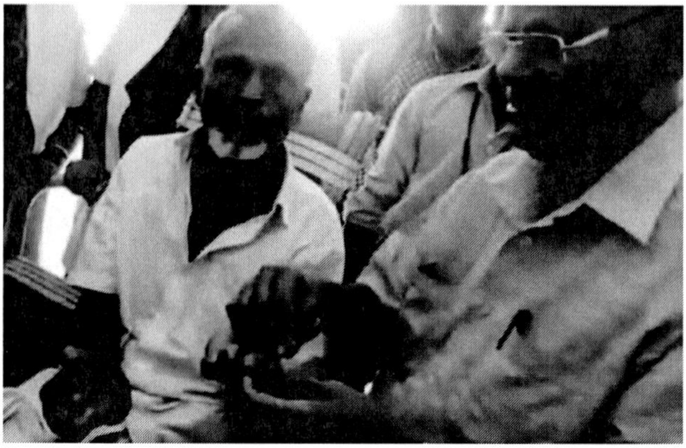

Leprosy patient class demonstration by Prof. N. Palani at Vinayaka missions medical collage Salem.

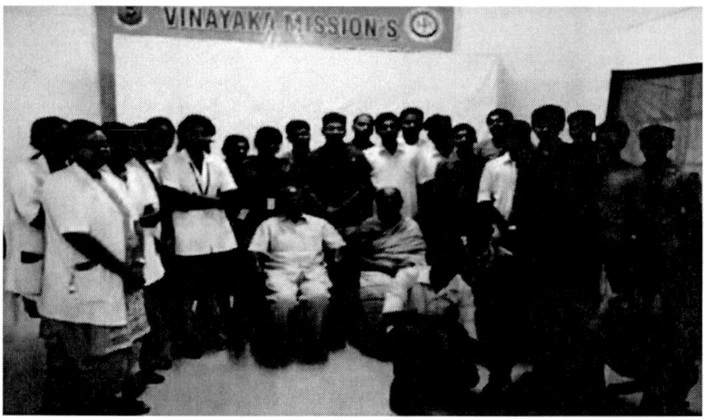

Fare Well Party by B.P.T Students.

Mr. Rajan Samuel , was appointed as the Principal and I continued as Director/college of Physiotherapy till July 2018. Rajan Samuel, the Principal , conducts a number of workshops and has modernized the education system here. He trains the students to take up social service. The academic coordinator, Mr. Sam Thamburaj, helps him in all respects.

It was indeed a great joy to have worked with eminent physiotherapists viz. , Mrs. Parker, Mr. Thomas Manickam,

Mr. John Samuel, Mr. Andrew Babu, Mr. Kerry Fry, Mr. Pasupathy, Mr. RajanSamuel, Mr. Basker, Mr. Perumal, Mr. Girivasan, Mr. Dhandapani, Mr. Erankumaran, Mr. Sam Thamburaj, Mr. Narayanan Mr. Karthigeyan, Mr. Anand, Mr. Furness, Mr. Vijayakumar, Miss. Mary Chidambaram, Mr. Vital Rao, Mrs. Mallika, Mr. Ramesh, Mr. SteveKolumban, Mr. Paul Namsivayan, Mr. Sengutuvel , Mr. Satish Kumar, Mr. Sudhakar, and others.

I also enjoyed working with Mr. Sadagopa N, Mr. N. Duraisamy, Mrs. Gandhibai, Mr. Kuppusamy, Mr. Dhanapal, Mr. Senthilkumar, Ms. Anandi, and others. I am also thankful to Dr. J. Richard for having helped me in the field of biostatistics for my paper presentations. His book on biostatistics and research methodology published by Prince Hall, Delhi, is in wide use. I also enjoyed the kindness shown by Dr. B. M. Puliood former principal cmc Hospital and Dr. H. H. S. Gass.

Mango Garden

The Vellore town where we lived the most, is famous for fresh vegetables and fruits. Every year, during the mango season, I would go to the mango market and buy large quantities of mangoes and ripe them in my house. Once it gets ripe, I enjoyed distributing these fruits to my family members and relatives.

I was always interested in the welfare of the environment and believed that planting trees would produce a lot of oxygen. Nevertheless, I could not do anything because of my stringent economic condition. Later on, after my retirement from Vellore, when I was freed from all my commitments, I started saving money while working at Vinayaga Missions and bought a small patch of 3 acres of land near Chengam and planted 300 mango trees on it. Now, the garden is really flourishing and has a good yield every year. I always prefer not to sell these mangoes, instead, I distribute them to the workers, relatives, and school children nearby and to the orphanages. The joy of giving has no bounds and one has to experience it to understand it.

My Diabetes

About 40 years ago, I was diagnosed with diabetes through a blood test. I was asked to have a restricted diet. For more than five years, I had managed without taking medicines. I had my diabetes under control by way of daily exercises and restricted diet. I adopted the following measures to have my blood sugar under control:

1) Monthly blood sugar test for diabetes
2) Avoiding sweets, cakes, and fruits
3) Taking small quantity of food four to five times a day
4) Taking medicine regularly
5) Walking and exercising regularly
6) Always working enthusiastically.
7) A diet with minimum carbohydrates
8) Avoid fasting
9) To go for periodical medical checkups

I was invited to deliver an address in a physiotherapy alumni association at CMCH, Vellore. I met an old student of mine there, who remarked, "Sir, you look the same as I saw you 25 years back! Whenever you entered the classroom, you used to look around in all directions to see whether the class room is clean. If you found a chalk piece or bits of paper anywhere, you yourself would pick it and put it in the dustbin. In the hospital, prayer starts sharp at 8. 00 am. You were always 5 minutes earlier for the prayer; you were never late. We learnt time management from you. "

Even at the age of 60, I used to go by cycle to the hospital, travelling a distance of6 km to and fro. Some people even told me, "For your status you can travel by car or by a two wheeler". I replied them by saying, "Bicycle is enough for me and if people respect me for my status; I do not worry about the others. Cycling is good for my health and I used to enjoy the rides greatly. Travelling by cycle is economical, keeps you healthy and is environment friendly".

I used to help the Physiotherapy course selection committee in all respects. The candidates were given written test, memory test and physical endurance test(lying down fast and then sitting immediately 25 times in a minute). My opinion is that physiotherapists must be physically strong and healthy in order to carry out their duty properly.

Some rare occurrences:

Once I was standing at a bus stand in Chennai. All of a sudden, I remembered waking up in a hospital Intensive Care Unit. As I had not taken diabetic medicines properly, I had fainted and fallen down in the same place due to hypoglycaemia. Some unknown person took pity on me and admitted me in a hospital. When I got well and opened my eyes, the doctor told me what had happened. From then onwards, I used to take my medicines properly and have periodic blood tests done and used to be very strict with my diet. Even in parties and functions like marriage, I avoid sweets. Because of this strict regime, I am able to have my diabetes in control and no major complication has happened to me because of diabetes.

One of my students was employed in leprosy hospital, Maharogi Seva Samithi, in which Mahatma Gandhi was interested. In one of his letters to me, he had mentioned as follows, "I do not know when I shall meet you again in my life time". In my reply to that letter, I had written that"I had planned to go to Delhi by train to attend a conference. If possible, you can meet me at Wardha railway station". Accordingly, he came to Wardha station along with two British friends and received me with a flower garland. I assured him that onmy return journey I would visit his hospital and offer the necessary assistance.

As per my assurance, I went to his hospital at Wardha during my return. I stayed therefor a few days and helped them in their work. Recently, I had been to Chengalpattu leprosy sanatorium where I had been treated for leprosy. The place had changed to a great extent in the last 70 years. All the old buildings had been removed. I went to see my boarding No. 6 where I stayed for the treatment. That particular building was still intact and I could remise my childhood days of struggle.

But standing there, at that moment, and thinking back, I had conquered leprosy. I did not develop any deformity of any sort, was more hale and healthy than my peers, had a very happy family with devoted and caring wife, I was able to bring up children to high positions and settle them well in life and contributed much for the cause of leprosy patients. I had acquaintance with very good people like Dr. Brand, Prof. T. N. Jagadeesan, Dr. Desikan, and could still keep active and work. This thought brought immense sense of joy and happiness to me.

The sanatoriums now less crowded and all the leprosy patients who stayed there were sent home after being treated with multi-drug therapy for leprosy. How true is Mahatma Gandhi's prophecy and his statement: donot invite me for opening of leprosy hospital but invite me for closing the same;has come true.

Conclusion:

In whatever endeavour I had undertaken, my wife was always with me. She hardly questioned my actions and always believed that what I did was for good. She never used to show any face or grumble if I bring people for lunch or dinner at home, although it meant so much of extra work for her. What impressed me the most was the unhitching devotion she had for me and my values. If I was free enough to go and work for leprosy related work, attend conferences, etc; it was all because she would take care of the family including my mentally upset mother. I remember every time I went from Katpadi to Delhi, she used to pack and bring my luggage in a town bus straight to the railway station whereas I used to finish my work at the hospital and go to the station without a thing to bother.

The relationship she shared with my sisters was the one to cherish. We always had some old relative or other taken care by her at our home. As my younger sister did not have children of her own, both she and her husband spent their last few months with us and passed away at our residence. All this was possible only because of my wife's sincerity and love for my family members.

Though I believe in God, I do not believe in any particular religion or ritual. Nor I have made myself attached with money. I believe that one should possess sufficient money to run a decent living and money need not be the top most priority in a person's life. That is the reason why I denied the various job offers from around the world and remained at CMCH, Vellore. Life has been good to me, blessed me with happiness and joy. I strongly believe that service to humanity is service to God

When you go through sufferings, you understand the suffering of others. Looking back at my life, I now think that if not for the leprosy I would have been another merchant at the Vellore market and could not have made any contribution to leprosy patients. Hence, I consider that leprosy was a blessing in my life rather than an obstacle.

Life is not a bed of roses without sufferings, rather it is the positive spirit and right approach that one should have to overcome obstacles and reach the destination. I am deeply distressed with the suicides of people and youth, especially those who commit to such extreme step when they face obstacles. One should stand up, accept challenges, and work with perseverance to overcome the obstacles. It is widely accepted that a society is run by its intelligentsia and if those people commit suicide, it is not a loss to them, but also to the society.

I would like to emphasize that our sole existence is in the hands of God. Our existence is nurtured and is a gift given by the society. To reciprocate this, we should contribute to the society as best as possible. We should be compassionate towards the downtrodden sections, care about environment, be kind to animals and work for the overall development of the society.

The most important person in the medical field is the patient and everything revolves around him. A patient looks up to a doctor and envisages him as an earthly God and hence the duty of a doctor is to treat the patient with single-minded devotion and not for any commercial interests.

It is said that the good of self is contained in the good of all. The society remembers only those who have served it, rather than the richest. It is evident from the life stories of Gandhi, Vivekananda, Mother Teresa, and many others.

The ultimate aim/destination of any human being on this Earth is to be happy, but only the means to achieve it are different for different people. I, being inspired by Gandhi and an ardent follower of him, advocate an austere, service-oriented, character-oriented, healthy, honest, disciplined and rational life, so as to live a happy and valuable life.

In conclusion, my message to people is to be brave at the time of adversity and work hard for the sake of self and nation. Frustrations and obstacles in our lives can be transformed through dedicated service to the Mankind which could elevate the spirit of the individual.

Pain Management:

The most important person in the medical field is the patient. Everything revolves around the patient and he should be given paramount importance during treatment with undivided attention. You should give him the best what you can.

Patients come to me with pain in their back, knee, and neck which occurs commonly due to ageing. After a few days of physiotherapy treatment, I suggest a home programme with hot water fermentation or by using an electric heating pad which is easily available for reduction of their pain. As per Vontoff's law, the heat produced in the tissue increases the blood supply and removes the waste products and thus helps in relieving the pain. This can be done easily at home. It is cost effective and the patient need not travel from one hospital to another hospital and spend money. The treatment can even be repeated 2 to 3 times a day at home to have better relief.

Those who have extensive damage in advanced conditions of the joints may go in for surgical intervention till which time this heat treatment can be an effective remedy along with exercise which includes certain dos and don'ts. Exercise is to be done within limits of pain, for about a minimum of 10 to 15 minutes daily.

1. Neck Pain

➢ Avoid bending of the neck for long hours.

➢ Don't carry heavy weight on the head.

➢ Don't carry heavy weights in arms.

➢ Avoid sagging pillows for the head, instead a tiny pillow or a towel can be used.

➢ For the relief of pain, heat treatment such as hot water fermentation, electric heating pad will be helpful.

➢ Avoid sleeping during the heat treatment.

Wrong (Big Pillow) Right(Small Pillow)

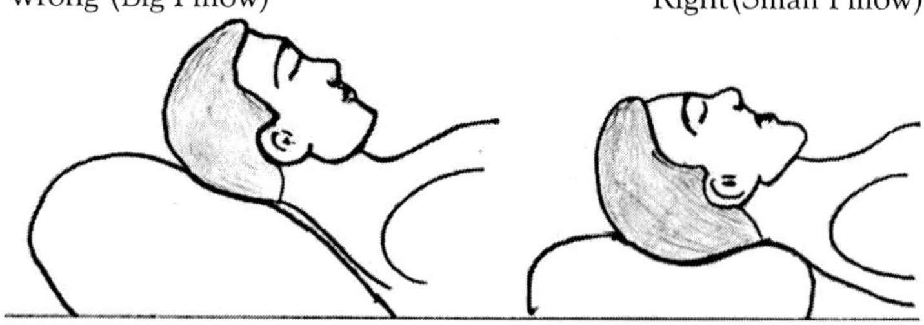

➢ An exercise program is given below:

Resistance exercise for the neck, as shown in the picture:

<u>PRESS AND RESIST</u>

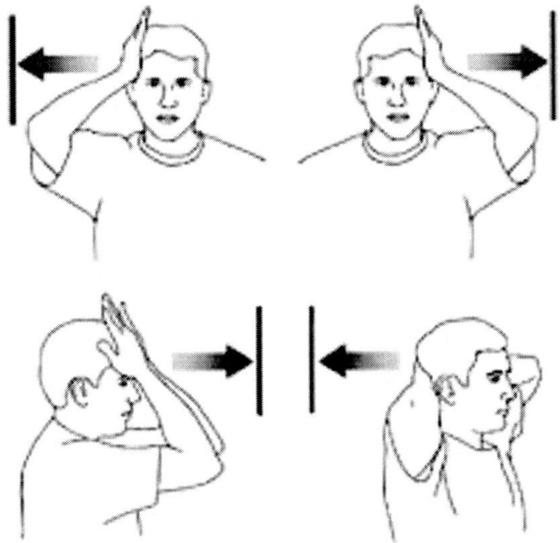

2. Lower back pain(Do's and Don'ts):

- Avoid bending the back and as far as possible, do all the work standing.
- Don't carry heavy weights.
- Use western toilets.
- Avoid sagging thick mattress instead use a thin mattress to sleep.
- Avoid floor level activities.
- For the relief of pain, heat treatment such as hot water fermentation, electric heating pad will be helpful.
- Avoid sleeping during the heat treatment.

- For intense pain, use a Lumbar Corset.
- Turn your body sideways, bend your legs and get up from the bed.
- Bend the knee while picking up objects from the floor
- Avoid two wheelers for travelling.
- Avoid sitting in the back seat of the bus, in order to prevent jerking/jolting.
- Do not run hurriedly to catch a bus or a train which may put strain to your back.

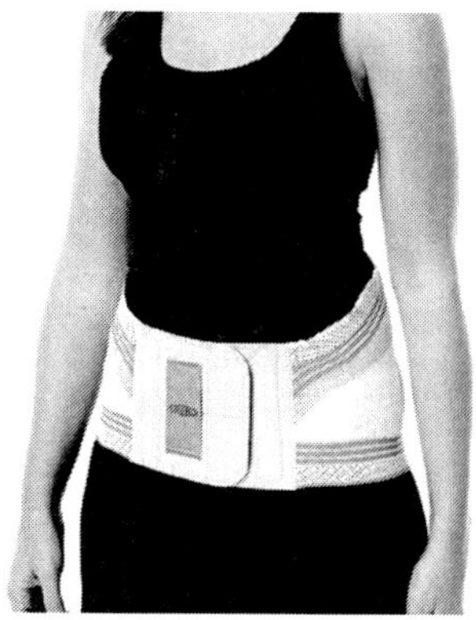

Resting position for low back pain

Exercises for low back pain

1 

2 

Lift up and down several times

3 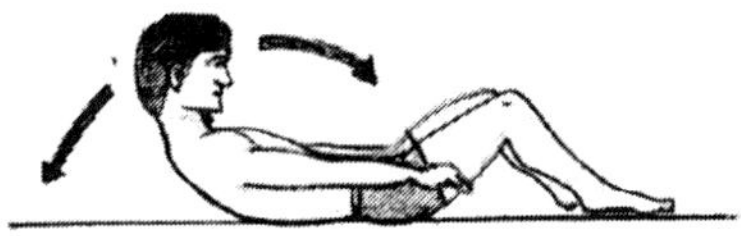

Back bending exercise up and down several times.

4 

Straight leg exercise without bending the knee.

5 

Face down lift up the leg up and down without bending the knee.

6 

Curl up the trunk up and down as shown in the picture several times.

3. Knee joint pain

- This is a common pain in the elderly age group. The wear and tear of knee joint can be progressive. In advanced conditions, the patient may require surgical treatment.
- Avoid prolonged standing
- Avoid climbing steep staircase
- If obese, reduce weight
- Avoid floor level activities
- Use western toilet
- Use rails for climbing staircase/ use the lift
- If pain persists, use a walking stick.
- Use knee cap, if needed.
- Exercise regularly.
- For the relief of pain, heat treatment such as hot water fermentation/ electric heating pad/wax bath will be helpful.

An exercise program for knee pain is given below:

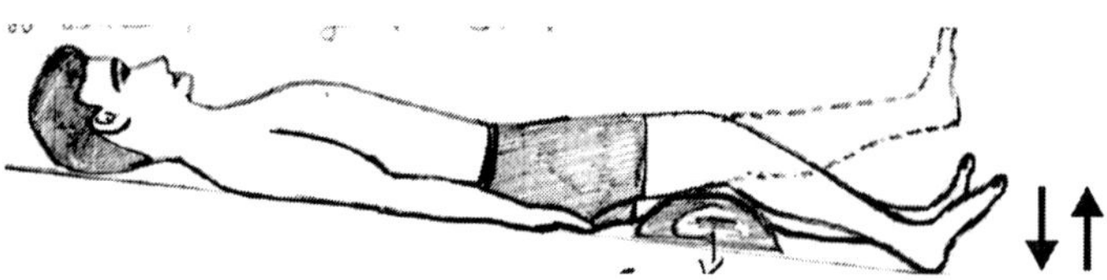

Big pillow under, knee up and down movement several times.

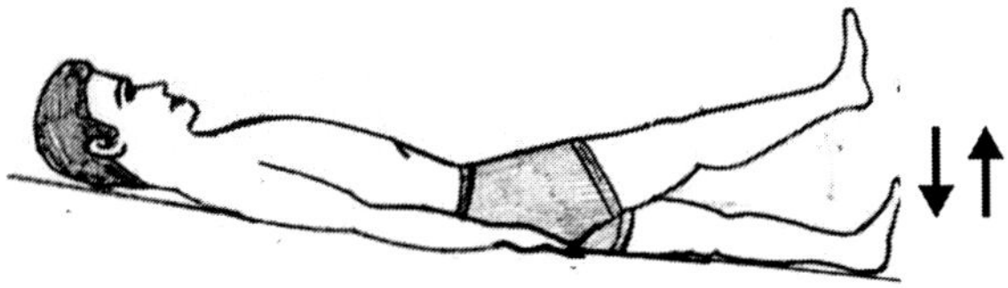

Straight leg exercise without bending the kneeseveral times.

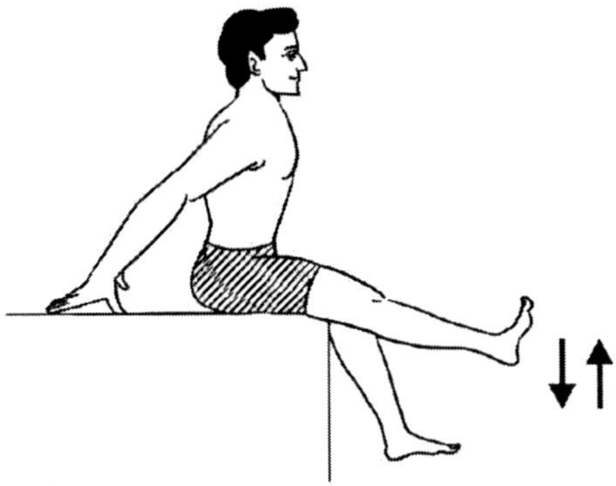

Lift the leg up and down several times, while sitting, keeping the knee straight.

One or two kgs
Strengthing exercise for the knee using weights as shown in the picture.

4. Shoulder Pain(Do's and Don'ts):

Elderly People are prone to shoulder pain. They can reduce the pain with the help of the following methods:

- Give hot water fermentation /electric heating pad, or wax bath in the place where there is pain;
- Exercise regularly;
- Avoid lifting heavy weights;
- Avoid sleeping with the head on the affected shoulder, which has pain.

An exercise program is given below:

These exercises can be done for 10 to 15 minutes, at least twice a day. For all these pains, medication on long term basis does not help very much and they also have side effects.

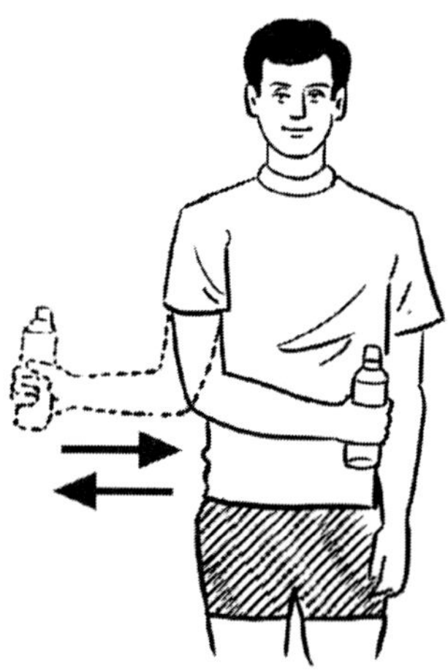

Water bottle, moving the arm as shown in the picture several times.

One or two kgs.
Lifting the arm with weight side ways movement.

Leaning on the table making a big circle as shown in the picture several times.

Crawling on the wall as shown in the picture several times.

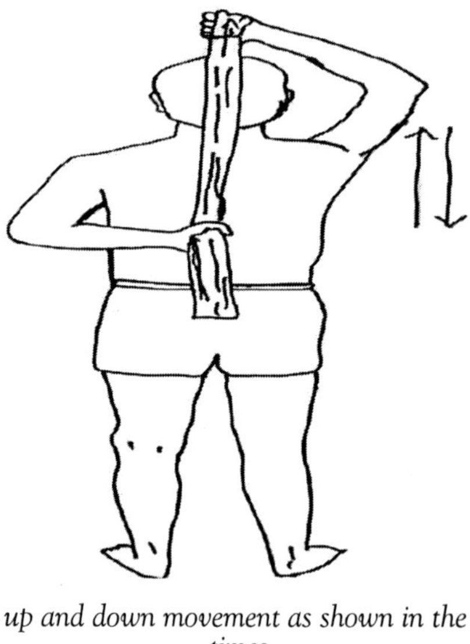

Hold a towel up and down movement as shown in the picture several times.

Obesity:

Obesity is one of the main causes for a number of ailments. Therefore, reduce your weight in order to maintain good health.

Obesity can also causes high blood pressure, heart ailments, and diabetes, etc.

To overcome obesity, avoid the following things;

(1) Sweet soft drinks

(2) Sweets

(3) High calorie non-vegetarian foods

(4) Root vegetables

(5) Oily foods

(6) Junk foods

(7) High Carbohydrate diets

(8) Alcohol and smoking to be avoided

(9) Obese patients, if they have a blood pressure should take regular treatment and avoid excess salty food such as pickles, papad, and ketchups, etc.

(10) Avoid bad habit of eating food frequently

(11) Avoid eating food in the middle of the night, in case you have finished dinner already.

Things to eat to reduce obesity -

(1) Vegetables

(2) Green leafy vegetables

(3) Pulses

(4) Egg white

(5) Food with less calorific value

(6) Eat food to fill three-fourth of the stomach capacity

(7) Do exercise and walk daily- it is a healthy habit.

Some quotes/hymns from Hinduism, Christianity, Buddhism, and Islam have been close to my heart and remained as the moral guidelines on which I have been trying to lay my whole life. I have reiterated them below:

Saint Vallarar's sayings:

1. Service to mankind is way to attain eternal peace.
2. Avoid contact with people who keep one thing in mind and talk differently to others.
3. Avoid telling lies.
4. Lead a healthy life free from illness.
5. Do not blindly follow any rituals.
6. Observe vegetarianism and avoid killing animals.

Strive to be happy (A Sanskrit Verse) from Vedas:

Na karmana na prajaya dhanena

Tyagenaike amirta tvamsuku

Immortality can be attained only by renunciation and not by achievements done in once lifetime or by acquiring wealth or by having a number of children.

Desiderata:

Desiderata (Latin: "desired things") is a 1927 prose poem by American writer Max Ehrmann. Largely unknown in the author's lifetime, the text became widely known after its use in a devotional, after being subsequently found on Adlai Stevenson's deathbed in 1965, and after spoken-word recordings in 1971 and 1972.

Go placidly amidst the noise and haste, and remember what peace there may be in silence. As far as possible, without surrender, be on good terms with all persons. Speak your truth quietly and clearly; and listen to others, even the dull and the ignorant; they too have their story.

Avoid loud and aggressive persons; they are vexatious to the spirit. If you compare yourself with others, you may become vain and bitter; for always there will be greater and lesser persons than yourself.

Enjoy your achievements as well as your plans. Stay interested in your own career, however humble. It is a real possession in the changing fortunes of time.

Exercise caution in your business affairs, for the world is full of trickery. But let this not blind you to what virtue there is; many persons strive for high ideals and everywhere life is full of heroism.

Be yourself. Do not feign affection. Neither be cynical about love, for in the face of all aridity and disenchantment, it is as perennial as the grass.

Take kindly the counsel of the years, gracefully surrendering the things of youth. Nurture strength of spirit to shield you in sudden misfortune. But do not distress yourself with dark imagining. Many fears are born of fatigue and loneliness.

Beyond a wholesome discipline, be gentle with yourself. You are a child of the universe, no less than the trees and the stars; you have a right to be here.

And whether or not it is clear to you, the universe is unfolding as it should. Therefore, be at peace with God, whatever you conceive Him to be, and whatever your labours and aspirations are, in the noisy confusion of life, keep peace with your soul. With all its shams, drudgery, and broken dreams, it is still a beautiful world. Be cheerful.

Quran (Islam):

Some of the verses from the Quran are given here:

Do not fight **WARS OF AGGRESSION**-[2:190]

There is **NO COMPULSION IN RELIGION**-[2:256]

Don't confuse **TRUTH** with **FALSEHOOD** or knowingly conceal the truth-[2:242]

GUARD YOUR OWN SOULS-[5:105]

SLAY NOT THE LIFE which Allah hath made sacred-[6:151]

Allah enjoy in the **JUSTICE** and **KINDNESS**, and **GIVING** to **KINSFOLK** and forbiddeth lewdness and abomination and wickedness-[16:90]

Be kind to PARENTS, RELATIVES, ORPHANS, the NEEDY, NEIGHBORS, and TRAVELERS-[4:36]

<u>Be kind to everyone</u> :

- Your kindness may be treated as weakness, Still be kind.
- Your help may go unnoticed, Still be helpful.
- If you are honest, People may cheat you, Be honest always.
- If you find happiness, they may be jealous, Be happy always.
- The good you do today, People will often forget tomorrow, Do good always.
- Because it is between you and ALLAH. It was never between you and them!

Christianity Hymn:

I need thee every hour Hymn

I need thee every hour, most gracious Lord;

no tender voice like thine can peace afford.

Refrain:

1. I need thee, O I need thee;
   every hour I need thee;
   O bless me now, my Savior, I come to thee.
2. I need thee every hour; stay thou nearby;
   temptations lose their power when thou art nigh.
   (Refrain)
3. I need thee every hour, in joy or pain;
   come quickly and abide, or life is vain.

(Refrain)

4. I need thee every hour; teach me thy will;

   and thy rich promises in me fulfill.

   (Refrain)

5. I need thee every hour, most Holy One;

   O make me thine indeed, thou blessed Son.

   (Refrain)

Lead Kindly Light Hymn

Lead, kindly Light, amid the encircling gloom, lead Thou me on!

The night is dark, and I am far from home; lead Thou me on!

Keep Thou my feet; I do not ask to see

The distant scene; one step enough for me.

I was not ever thus, nor prayed that Thou shouldst lead me on;

I loved to choose and see my path; but now lead Thou me on!

I loved the garish day, and, spite of fears,

Pride ruled my will. Remember not past years!

So long Thy power hath blest me, sure it still will lead me on.

O'er moor and fen, o'er crag and torrent, till the night is gone,

And with the morn those angel faces smile, which I Have loved long since, and lost a while!

Meantime, along the narrow rugged path, Thyself hast trod, Lead, Savior, lead me home in childlike faith, home to my God.

To rest forever after earthly strife
In the calm light of everlasting life.

Thirukural

Avoid an act which you may repent later; If done by mistake, better not to repeat it. (Kural No. : 655)

True friends guard you from evil, make you walk in right path and share your sorrows in difficult times. (Kural No. : 787)

The learned teacher makes you enjoy learning; On leaving, makes you to keep thinking of his teaching. (Kural No. : 394)

Think and then undertake the work; to think after commencement will bring disgrace. (Kural No. : 467)

Determined efforts result in prosperity; Idleness will bring nothing. (Kural No. : 616)

Let the thoughts be always great and progressive. It will not be a loss, even if the success eludes. (Kural No. : 596)

Buddha's teachings:

The cause of suffering: The Buddha explained that people live in a sea of suffering because of ignorance and greed. They are ignorant of the law of karma and are greedy for the wrong kind of pleasures.

The end of suffering: To end suffering, one must cut off greed and ignorance.

Right Livelihood. This means choosing a job that does not hurt others. The Buddha said, "Do not earn your living by harming others. Do not seek happiness by making others unhappy. "

Right Effort. A worthwhile life means doing our best at all times and having good will toward others. This also means not wasting effort on things that harm ourselves and others.

QUOTES OF MAHATMA GANDHI:

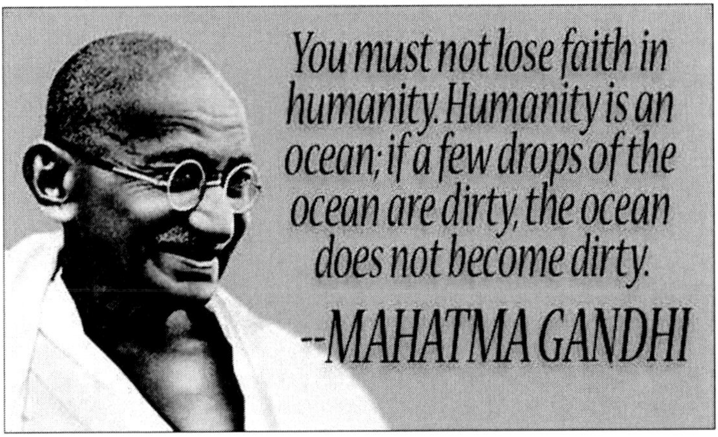

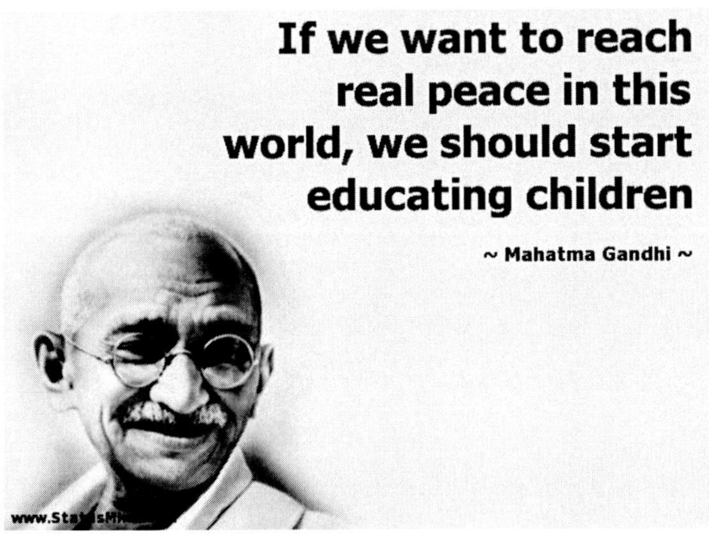

"You must be the change you wish to see in the world."

BIBLIOGRAPHY:

My experiments with truth by M. K. Gandhi

Ten Fingers for God by Dorothy Clarke Wilson

The Gift of Pain by Dr. Paul Brand & Philip Yancey

Take my Hands by Dorothy Clarke Wilson

In his Image by Dr. Paul Brand & Philip Yancey

Leprosy in Theory and Practice by Dr. R. G. Cochrane

Doctor Ida Scudder by Dorothy Clarke Wilson

Navajeevan Publication House, Ahamedabad.

Thadaikalle padikal [TAMIL] Prof. N. Palani

WHO Reports